Echoes from the Mountains

Pauline Hensley Harber

Dedications

For Emily Stidham, the great, great granddaughter and the only namesake of Grandmother Emily Smith.

For Della Mae Hensley who was born in the early forties but has lived her life at the foot of Brush Mountain in a remote area, experiencing a similar life to Grandmother Emily who was born in 1878. Della Mae has fulfilled the calling on her life as a strong mountain woman. Her trials have been many, but, like Emily, she has been and is a survivor.

In memoriam of my loving daughter, Kimberly Lynn Harber, a high school teacher who loved the mountains that brought peace to her soul as she rode her Arabian horse through the mountains, hills and streams, strong and free.

Special thanks to Rhonda Robinson for her unending support.

This book is dedicated to all of Grandmother Emily's generations.

Chapter 1

Sunrays glowed softly through the trees as the tender green leaves fluttered from the late March winds, sending chills through the bodies of Malachi and Grace Hensley as they journeyed from North Carolina into Brush Mountain, nestled in the corner where Kentucky, Tennessee, and Virginia meet. Their plan was to settle on the Kentucky side. The trail they walked could only accommodate horses and other animals as well as people. They were only able to bring bare necessities.

"Grace, I am very thankful we were able to bring the things we need to start over."

Grace was in deep thought as she was mesmerized by the beauty of the mountains. Her chest felt like it would burst right open it was so full of joy. A heartfelt peace swept gently through her soul like the cool clear water of the wild river that flowed from Brush Mountain down to the valley, winding its way to Martin's Fork River and on to the big Cumberland. Of course, Grace had no concept then of the valley below or the Wild River.

After many hours of walking it was as if a huge curtain had suddenly dropped, turning daylight into near dark.

"Grace, we had better find a level spot to hold up for the night."

"Malachi, look! There's a flat spot right over there we can tie our horses to a tree and stay for the night."

As they lay looking toward the stars that night, Grace felt a little frightened but hid her feelings. She eased from the quilt they lay on. She was not able to sleep in an environment that was so strange to her. The fire glowed and the flames flickered and danced as Grace sat staring into them.

She sat wondering what the end of their journey would be like. Her thoughts traveled a million miles as she sat there by the fire, occasionally laying a dead branch gathered from the ground of the surrounding woods on it to keep the flame alive.

Finally she snuggled behind Malachi, her dark haired, blue-eyed Prince Charming. She continued to wonder what their destiny would be in Brush Mountain as the heat of the fire warmed her towards sleep. She knew from Malachi's stories that his great grandfather had experienced life in Brush Mountain many years ago. It would be a different world from what she had known but she was willing to walk beside her man no matter where it would take her. She resolved to find all the strength in her heart to endeavor on regardless of what her fate might be.

'I will be strong like an eagle. I will fly no matter how many times I fall,' she vowed to herself.

They awoke to look upon the eastern sky as the sun rose above the hills.

"Grace, you will see many sunrises unlike any you have ever seen."

Malachi looked upon Grace as she stood staring toward the rising of the sun. As he studied her beautiful face, flawless skin and long dark hair, he thought, 'I've been too busy in North Carolina to notice the fullness of my own wife's beauty.' Even in a long flannel nightgown with no makeup, she was a natural beauty. Malachi's heart was warmed and at that moment he knew he would labor hard to make a good life for his lovely Grace. Malachi honored her meek and humble spirit. As he looked at her the thought of one of the Proverbs; the words seemed to flow through him and take root in his heart: 'Who can find a virtuous woman? For her price is far above rubies. The heart of her husband doth safely trust in her so that he shall have no need of spoil, she will do him good and not evil all the days of her life.'

Malachi moved from the rock he sat on and stood to face his Grace. "You are so beautiful in the mornings." He gently raised her face toward his with a fingertip beneath her chin. "Grace, everything will be good for us, I promise. We will grow old together."

There was a sadness in Grace's eyes that concerned Malachi, but he knew she had not slept well and was tired from their journey.

6

Malachi took dried apples and shelled walnuts from the saddle bags. Walking to the nearby stream, he filled the coffeepot and brought it back to the fire. He stacked rocks together with embers between them and placed the coffeepot on them to boil.

As he worked, he watched as Grace walked down to the clear stream and knelt to splash cool water over her beautiful olive skin before changing into a fresh cotton dress. She combed her long, dark hair then made her way back to camp seeming more rejuvenated and ready to continue their journey.

After breakfast was eaten and cleared away, they were ready to complete their journey to the unknown land.

Spring was in the air; the breeze warmer than the day before. Birds flew about in abundance, singing from the treetops. The sight was uplifting and helped Grace put away her thoughts of the night before.

After walking for a few hours, they stopped for a rest and a snack of leftover breakfast. When they were finished, Malachi gently took Grace into his arms.

"Grace, all will be well."

"I know that, Malachi."

As the day passed, Grace realized she believed what she had told her husband. She felt her spirit lifted with every step. She almost felt bubbly inside, which also improved Malachi's spirits.

As they neared Brush Mountain, they could see it from the ridge where they stood. "Look, Malachi, look, See how flat the top of that mountain is."

Malachi nodded. "Look at the rolling land between, and the flat benches in the mountains."

"Oh, Malachi, this is more than I ever dreamed of."

"I pledge to you and to God: I will work hard. I will be by your side doing whatever I need to do."

"Malachi, do you think there are other settlers in that beautiful mountain?"

"There must be, Grace. We can't possibly be the first to follow their dreams into this God-given land."

As they ended their long journey, their hearts overflowed with joy and peace. The tiredness and discouragement experienced over the long trip flowed away. Grace could tell Malachi was excited and she was as well.

When they reached a meadow of rippling, green grass, she just knew. "Malachi, this is our spot! We'll build a big log cabin here, beginning with one great big room."

Malachi was nodding. "We'll build a smokehouse, a barn, and a root cellar over there beyond that big oak tree." He turned around to the place Grace had picked for the cabin. "I'll build a huge rock fireplace and put a window on each side."

"When you can, I want pale yellow cloth to sew curtains. In the warm weather, the breeze will let them flow back into the room and in the winter, the color will remind me of the sun. Will we be able to walk or ride a horse to a store from here?"

"I can take the trail by horseback to North Carolina. If I go to bed early and sleep a few hours, I can leave about one in the morning and be back not long after dark. I can make the trip back for what we need from time to time."

"Maybe once we meet other people, we'll learn of a store that's closer."

As the excitement subsided, Grace realized there were some things to be considered. She had managed to bring a setting hen that would need a place to nest. She spotted a huge tree with a big hollow spot on one side that would be perfect for a temporary nest. She made her way to it and placed dried leaves inside. She had brought fertile eggs in a feather pillow to keep them safe. Placing them in the nest, she finally untied the legs of the big Rhode Island Red hen and delicately sat her on the nest, then carefully placed the eggs beneath her. The hen fluffed her feathers over the eggs to cover them.

She walked back to Malachi who was busy finding a place for their supplies. "Before winter comes on, she'll hatch diddles time and again. We'll eat mostly roosters so the pullets will grow and lay eggs of their own. We'll get more and more chickens. Not only will they be food for us all year round, we can do so much with the eggs. I'll save feathers and you can get me some ticking cloth to make a feather bed. If I can save enough feathers, I'll make one for a cover too, so we can sleep on one and under one."

As Grace was talking about her plans, Malachi was carefully studying the land. "Grace, let's walk over that little hill."

Holding hands as they walked, they were pleased to find a piece of ground beyond the hilltop that would be perfect for their crops.

"We'll clean up that ground, Grace, and call it our new ground." Walking across the field, Malachi kicked the soil with his boot. "Look how rich that earth is, we can grow all kinds of vegetables to eat, and corn to feed the livestock." Food was the main concern of every settler. Along with their horses, they had brought a Jersey cow through the mountains and one small pig in a burlap sack, squirming and squealing the whole way. Of course their dog had followed along, he was a mutt, but a fine watchdog and they loved him.

"Malachi, we really are blessed. I believe God has ordered our steps."

Returning to the house seat where they would soon raise their cabin, they were filled with hope.

"Let's walk over to the other side." Grace was so excited she walked ahead of her husband barely containing her enthusiasm. "Malachi, hurry! Look at that stream of water, how it bubbles and runs over the rocks as it comes off the ridge."

"Grace, look! Look at the very top. It comes right out of the ground and rocks. I bet it never goes dry."

"Malachi! See the redbud, dogwood and wild flowers growing by the water. I have never seen anything that pretty." Spring had come early and the trees were in full bloom.

Darkness finally began to hover over the mountains and its beauty as they explored. This would be their first night in their newfound land, where Grace hoped they would settle permanently. They slept under the stars on a quilt laid over soft leaves. The night was clear and a little cool, but they could hear the sounds of whippoorwills, hoot owls, screech owls and the distant bark of a fox. A train whistle echoed all the way over from Virginia. The soothing sounds sent them off to a peaceful sleep, dreaming of all the things they would do in the morning.

As daylight filtered in through the trees, Malachi rose and stacked rocks around their fire. He sat the iron skillet across the rocks and prepared to fry fritters and ham. He filled the coffeepot from their stream and put it on to boil. The smells of sizzling ham and perking coffee finally roused Grace, who had slept deeply. She gave him a smile as she moved off to the stream to refresh herself.

As they ate, Grace smiled reassuringly at Malachi. "Let the fire keep burning and I'll put some beans on to cook in the small iron pot for supper. Tomorrow, I'll hunt fresh greens from the mountains."

Malachi nodded. "Today we should build a lean-to. We can cut some small poles to build two sides and a top that we can cover with the tar paper we brought in case it rains. It'll be big enough to sleep under and keep the supplies dry while we start on the cabin."

They finished breakfast and Malachi stood. "I'll be over there where the trees are plentiful. I'll start chopping them down for our lean-to and cabin."

Malachi set to work chopping strong, straight trees. After a while, he saw someone approaching.

"Howdy! I'm Nathaniel, but call me Nate." With sandy hair and dark blue eyes, Nate was a strong, healthy man of medium, muscular build.

"Sure is good to meet someone up here. I'm Malachi."

"I live not too fer down the mountain. When did you make it to these parts?"

"We got here yesterday, about mid-afternoon."

"Well, Malachi, I already got my seed in the ground, so I have a lot of free time right now. I'll be glad to help you build yer cabin. I like staying busy and helping others as the Good Book tells us to."

Malachi thought about how difficult it would be for Grace to help with the logs. "Nate, I'd be obliged to have your help."

The men accomplished a lot that day, working until the April sun finally started to set. Nate returned every day and they worked hard until Malachi felt he should leave off the tree cutting and get his seeds in the ground. It was already a little late for some of the crops to grow well, but Malachi was confident they would raise plenty to live on. He had not been able to bring seed potatoes, which worried him a little. Nate brought some from his previous crop. The help Nate extended was more than Malachi could ever have hoped for.

The day before planting, after the men had cleared the ground, Grace cooked dinner of fresh mountain greens seasoned with side pork, fried corn bread, and, of course, beans. The men seemed to enjoy their dinner to the fullest.

Nate promised, "Grace, I will bring Ruth up tomorrow."

Grace looked forward to having a new friend.

The next day, Nate brought up his bull-tongue plow to lay off the rows for planting and Ruth came with him. Ruth was a beautiful woman with blond hair, blue eyes, and fair skin. Grace could tell Ruth was not afraid of hard work.

They pitched in to help the men and they got all their seeds in just before the warm spring rain began to fall. Grace raised her eyes to the sky and thanked God for this blessing.

She invited Nate and Ruth to stay for supper, knowing Ruth would be tired after the long day's work.

Brush Mountain

The Wild River

Malachi and Grace's granddaughter, Ruthie, and her children visiting their ancestral home on Brush Mountain

Hensley Settlement

Wild River nearing Martin's Fork

Wild River

Chapter 2

It was a beautiful clear day, the sky was blue with downy
clouds gently floating above the mountains. Malachi and Grace had
just finished breakfast when they heard men's voices. Looking down
the mountain, Grace recognized Nate but no one else.

Nate came up with a smile. "Malachi, this is Will, Richard,
and Jerrod. They want to help with your cabin."

Grace and Malachi were overcome with gratitude, this was
nothing short of a miracle. All he could say was, "I thank all of you."

Ruth came later in the morning to help Grace cook for the
men, bringing food left from their harvest the year before. She had
shuck beans, potatoes, cabbage, apples, and more. The women spent
the entire morning cooking and talking of the past and their future
hopes.

When the men came for dinner, they enjoyed it immensely.
The cold sweet milk kept cool in the spring delighted them.

Within a few days the trees were all cut and moved to the
house site. By the end of July, even the big rock fireplace was
finished, with windows on each side, just as Malachi had promised.

Grace and Ruth cooked a big celebration dinner and Will,
Jerrod, and Richard brought their wives. The neighbors were
generous, bringing Grace iron pots and other needed items she had
been unable to bring with her. The biggest surprise of all was that
each woman brought Grace enough feathers to finish her feather
mattress. The men had already built the bed frame.

After everyone left, Grace was so grateful the tears slid down
her face as freely as the clear water of their stream. She felt she had
been rewarded by God for being willing to work without complaint.
Their new neighbors had been so wonderful, she knew she could not
have helped Malachi so much.

Later that week, Ruth came for a visit and brought flower
seeds and starts. "Grace, these bleeding hearts bloom into a pink

heart and look as though a drop of blood is attached to the white center. We can plant the zinnias near the house, they're tall and bloom in all colors. Pink is my favorite. We can make a bed for the red sage in the middle of the yard. They bloom all summer and fall."

They stacked rocks in a circle to create a border for the flower bed. Ruth had also brought morning glory seeds which they planted near the smokehouse so the vines would climb the poles. Grace looked forward to seeing them bloom on summer mornings.

"Ruth, I can't thank you enough for all you've done for me. I love sitting outside in the morning and I know I'll enjoy looking at all the fresh blooms while I sip my coffee."

By the time Nate and Malachi came from working on the barn, Grace and Ruth had the flowers planted and dinner ready. The women enjoyed each others' company while the barn was being built. By the time it was done, it was time for crops to be tended so the woman did not see each other as often.

Grace and Malachi worked from dawn to dark tending their garden, building a pig run and a hen house with nests. They dug a cellar back into the ground with shelves made from smaller split logs for storing their winter food. They were able to get starts of cherry and apple trees and hope they would bear the following spring.

Malachi made occasional trips back to North Carolina to bring back needed supplies, especially cloth. Grace was very good at sewing, able to make almost anything by hand. By the time winter came, she would be well stocked with sewing goods.

Spring and summer passed swiftly into November. They were really busy with building, planting, harvesting, and preserving. They went to visit Nate and Ruth when they could, but they were busy as well preparing for winter. The pig had grown to a huge sow with piglets. The sow would be fattened once the piglets were weaned and slaughtered for their winter meat. They would salt the meat and hang it in the smokehouse. The piglets would grow and breed, so they would never need to worry about needing pork. They would be able to have a hog slaughter every winter to help themselves and their neighbors get through until spring. In the summer, they would depend on the chickens for meat and eggs.

16

"Well, Grace, think about all we've accomplished in three seasons: a fine cabin, a barn, a corn crib, a cellar, a hog run, a hen house, a good bed, a table with benches, a wood shed and plenty of wood. And your yellow curtains."

"We mustn't ever forget our wonderful friends, Malachi. They were a Godsend."

"God has been good to us, and I am thankful, Grace."

Grace and Malachi joined their work-worn hands together and lay them on the bible, giving thanks for all the strength to accomplish all they had so far.

"Lord, we now thank you that our bodies can receive rest throughout the winter here on Brush Mountain to prepare for the seasons to come. Amen and amen. And God bless our generations to come."

As Malachi and Grace lay snuggled into the soft feather bed under cool muslin sheets and Grace's homemade quilts, they were relaxed and warm as the snow piled up outside. It was comforting to look out through the window as the snow flakes floated down, knowing they were safe in their new home and ready for the winter.

The winter was long and cold, snowfall followed snowfall, but Malachi kept busy tending to the animals and bringing in wood, while Grace sewed, cleaned, and cooked.

The thaw came early in 1877, by March spring was already in the air. The streams were flowing swiftly down the mountains as melting snow poured into them. By this time their food supply was getting low, but they knew how to survive on what was left and what the mountain could provide until they could plant the gardens to bring forth new, fresh food. Malachi hunted wild game while Grace picked fresh greens from the mountains. She had learned early on which greens were edible. They still had a few dried beans and extra potatoes not reserved for planting.

Again, Malachi and Grace worked hard all three seasons to prepare for another winter. Their gardens yielded a plentiful crop and the animals thrived which would provide them plenty of pork and poultry. A new calf was born in the spring and it wasn't long until they would have fresh milk and butter. Malachi had built a spring house over the cold spring to keep their food fresh and cool.

Many in the mountains felt that the color of wooly worms helped predict how rough a winter would be. The different shades of brown told how long and how bad the weather could get. One day Nate and Malachi were hunting when the subject came up.

"Malachi, this winter coming is going to be a rough one. I've judged it before by the wooly worm's color."

"I believe you, Nate. I've heard talk of it before but never watched to see if it turned out right."

By mid-October the trees had turned every color imaginable. Grace loved the luminous gold and crimson red maples that almost looked like they were on fire.

Ruth and Grace took peaceful walks in the fall while the men hunted. They absorbed all the beauty around them, watching the leaves sail through the air under the azure skies.

"Grace, I've been here as long as I can remember and never longed to leave the mountains. Where in this world could we find anything as beautiful? I've heard tell of big cities and towns, but don't want no part of them. I believe you'll grow to love it as much as I do."

"Ruth, I have never been happier in my life. I want to spend the rest of my life here, even if I live a hundred years."

The women enjoyed each others friendship to the fullest, gathering seeds from their flower beds to plant in the spring while the men were gone hunting.

As autumn approached, Grace realized she was with child. She didn't voice it to anyone, not even Ruth. She feared Ruth would prevent her from helping with the winter preparations.

After Nate and Ruth headed home one evening, Malachi and Grace went inside. The cool October air breezed through the house making Grace a little sad. She knew it would be four months or more before fresh air would stir through the cabin again. Grace loved nature and knew she could slide her curtains back and see the rain and snow fall. This made her feel a little better about autumn giving way to winter.

Grace put supper on the table and they ate. Malachi smiled, his way of letting her know she was a good cook. Once the table was cleared, Malachi called her to sit with him by the fire.

As they sat by the hearth, Grace felt a bit nervous. She knew it was time to tell Malachi her news.

"Malachi… we have a little one on the way. It should be here about the time spring sets in, probably in March."

Malachi put his arm around Grace and held her close to reassure her he was happy and that all was well. Grace felt so loved and peaceful in that moment just to see the look of excitement on his face.

"Grace, I'll try to get cloth for you to sew this winter so our baby will have what it needs."

In the 1800s in the mountains babies both male and female wore white gowns for the first months, so materials would be no problem. Small blankets could be made from store bought flannel and socks could be knitted. Come summer, she would need cotton to make clothes appropriate to the sex of the child. Grace was a good seamstress by hand and, perhaps, someday she would have a treadle sewing machine.

"Grace, since we will be likely to have spare time when everything is frozen up here on the mountain, while you're busy sewing, I'll be busy making a wooden cradle."

"Thank you, Malachi. I know we'll be a good mommy and daddy."

"We'll do the best we can."

"I've pondered on names for the baby. If we have a girl, I want to call her Emily, but if it's a boy, I'd be honored if you name him."

Chapter 3

Malachi and Grace were both of Cherokee descent from their grandparents in Buncomb County, North Carolina. Malachi's father, William Burton Hensley had been born in Yancy county, North Carolina, Malachi felt he had inherited some of his father's looks, but Grace showed her Cherokee blood in a truly rare mixture. Her name described her perfectly. Knowing he was to be the father of her children made him happier than ever in his life. Brush Mountain became more and more their home as they adjusted to the knowledge they would soon be parents.

This winter was much colder than the first. The days were long and dreary, but Grace seemed peaceful. She smiled all the time as she did her chores.

Grace dreamed of her baby. If it was a girl, would it look like her? She had so many questions inside. Every time she felt her baby move inside, it made her heart leap with joy. She prayed she would be the best mother possible and hoped Malachi would never change. She wanted to give her child the best life could offer and nurture it through the years to become all it could hope for. She wondered if the child would grow up and leave the mountains some day as she had left her home. She knew in her heart that she could not impose her dreams on her child, that it would follow its own destiny.

The blizzards of winter finally passed and spring was just around the corner. On March 17, 1878, Grace awakened to a cold, windy morning feeling odd.

"Malachi? Will you go for Ruth? I think it's time."

Malachi looked surprised and nervous, but dressed hurriedly, smiling the whole time. Grace felt her own apprehension ease.

"I'll be there and back before you know it. Just be calm. And whatever you do, Grace, don't have this baby until I get back."

She smiled to reassure him and he flew out the door.

Malachi was so excited he began yelling when still a fair distance from Nate and Ruth's. "Ruth, it's time! Nate, get your horse!"

Ruth and Nate hurried as fast as they could and within minutes they were moving up the mountain filled with worry and anticipation.

"Go faster, Nate!"

"Ruth, our horse is doing his best. I'm sure he's nervous too!"

Grace had been busy while Malachi was gone, water was boiling and everything was ready: the scissors to cut the navel cord danced a little in the bottom of the pan. She had placed a clean cloth by the bed to tie the cord off once it was cut. Clean sheets, with padding beneath to protect the feather bed were in place.

Ruth entered the cabin yelling back at the men. "Nate, you and Malachi wait outside, I'll call if I need you."

Ruth had delivered babies before and Grace knew she sometimes felt sad because she had never conceived. Ruth felt there had to be some logic as to why she had never conceived a child, she believed in God's timing.

Grace lay down on the bed. She was strong and tried to be brave as she followed Ruth's directions. She made low sounds in her throat as the pain ebbed and flowed. When the cry of the baby finally pierced the quiet, she heard Malachi let out a yell from somewhere outside. Grace was sure both the cry and the yell could be heard a ridge away, echoing across and back again.

"You have a little girl, Grace!"

Tears slid down her face and Grace finally got her first look at her baby. She looked just like Grace had dreamed, a black haired baby girl with blue eyes. "I will call her Emily," she said, smiling as she wiped the tears from her face.

"Oh, Grace, she looks just like you. Just beautiful."

Ruth bathed Emily, washing her thick black hair before pinning a soft cloth diaper on her and dressing her in a white gown. She wrapped the baby in a yellow flannel blanket then laid her on Grace's stomach. Finally, she opened the door.

"Malachi! Nate! It's a beautiful little girl. Come and see!"

Malachi fought back tears of joy. He smiled as his heart filled with happiness. Little Emily had all the Cherokee traits of his and Grace's families, with vivid blue eyes.

Ruth cooked supper and made sure Grace was doing well before leaving. She came every day for nine days to lend a helping hand with Emily. She had cared for many babies and mommas over the years. She and Grace enjoyed long talks as Ruth cleaned and cooked, stopping occasionally for tea made from mountain herbs. Malachi and Nate were out planting early spring vegetables: beets, onions, peas and potatoes.

When she was recovered, Grace was soon busy taking care of her little Emily and doing her housework. Before she knew it, her baby was already nearly a month old. She took walks with Emily snuggled in her arms, enjoying the blooming of the redbuds. She sometimes wondered why they were called redbuds when they were actually more a pinkish purple. The trees were abundant in the mountains and by the end of April were loosing their blooms, the colorful petals drifting to the ground like snow near the little wild flowers bursting through the rich soil near the stream. Grace would talk to Emily as if she understood everything she was saying. Emily's eyes seemed to take in everything.

Brush Mountain became more and more comfortable. More people began to settle in the mountains, a family here, a family there, but the population was still sparse. The months passed swiftly and Emily was walking before Christmas of 1878. Their third Christmas on the mountain was different from others.

Malachi cut a fine hemlock for their Christmas tree and set it to the right of the fireplace. Grace decorated it with holly leaves and berries, making a holly berry rope with thread and green bows. Malachi made a trip to shop for Emily and Grace as he had been able to sell a few hogs and a calf, plus some extra vegetables from the gardens. Their first Christmas with Emily was the best they had ever known.

The years passed all too quickly as Grace nurtured her child to the best of her ability. She asked Malachi to purchase bible storybooks for her to read to Emily as they sat by the fire or beneath the blooming cherry tree in the yard. Emily was always by Grace's side as she did her chores, pretending to help in the garden or to milk the cow. Every Christmas Grace would tell Emily of the birth of Jesus and hold her up to search for the special star through the window. Memories were being made that Emily would carry all the days of her life.

Emily loved the little bed her dad built for her on the other side of the room. Grace had sewn beautiful curtains to create some privacy. At times, when Emily fretted after a confusing dream, Grace would lie down beside her. She made matching dresses for them both.

Emily's hair grew long and straight, just like her mother's and the older she grew, the more she looked like Grace. The key difference being Emily was a little more high-spirited than her mother. At the age of four, she would have ridden a horse if Grace and Malachi had turned her loose. Sometimes, if she was persistent enough, Malachi would walk the horse as Emily sat in the saddle.

Malachi adored both his girls.

Grace became ill in the early part of winter, so sick that Malachi went for help. Ruth and Nate were well versed in the mountain medicinal plants and soon had Grace well again. They were so grateful, they invited their friends for Christmas.

Ruth made presents for Emily: a beautiful doll and doll clothes. Nate made a tiny cradle for the doll. Grace had sewn matching clothes for Emily and her doll. Nate and Malachi got a warm knitted scarf. For Ruth she made pillowcases and a table cloth stitched with spring flowers. Working to get through the winter had been hard, but Grace made the time to create gifts for her family and friends.

Presents were opened early so Emily would not have to wait. The little girl just knew Santa had been there.

As the turkey roasted in the coal burning cook stove Nate and Ruth had given them, Grace made apple and cherry pies from the fruit she had canned earlier in the year. Ruth had cooked shuck beans with cured bacon the night before and brought them for their feast. Grace covered her table with a fine white tablecloth she had embroidered with the green leaves and red berries of the holly trees around her home. The fire glowed cheerily as the snow fell outside. It was the perfect Christmas setting.

Emily was asked to pray before dinner and said, "I thank you God for Baby Jesus that was born on Christmas Day."

With an 'amen' all around, they enjoyed their dinner. Afterward they sat around the fire and talked of their blessings, making plans to spend the next Christmas together. As Emily played with her new doll and cradle, the adults prayed more blessing would come in the intervening year.

As winter faded, spring came on before they even realized. In March, Emily turned five and by April the trees were budding again. Emily began to see her home through different eyes. She loved the mountains and had never seen any other place. This was her world: she knew no other.

As the berries began to ripen, she found tasty treats not far from home. Mulberries, from the trees down by the new ground, were her favorite. She thought the long, wine-colored berries were the best thing she had ever tasted. She would sit under the tree and eat them for what seemed an eternity.

It seemed like every day she would encounter some new bounty of the mountains. Wild grapes, persimmons, sour grass, raspberries, ground cherries… the mountains were full of wonderful things.

Emily loved watching the birds come to share in the fruit of the mountains. The red cardinals, Carolina bluebirds, and bright yellow orioles swooped around each other, flitting from branch to branch.

She would sit and observe the many other tiny creatures of the forest for hours. The squirrels would chitter as they carried their harvest of hickory nuts and black walnuts to their secret hiding places. Rabbits would scurry through the underbrush grazing from succulent green plants to dropped fruit or even vegetables from Malachi's garden.

Emily would watch her father go off into the hills and return with deer, pheasant, turkey, or sometimes even a wild goose. Her mountains provided everything she could ever want or need, and her mother and father made sure she wanted for nothing. She never felt lonely.

Chapter 4

On a morning in late April 1883, the air was still as the fog settled into the hollows between the ridges. The sun crept above the treetops, rays of soft warm light filtered through the branches sending dappled color into the hidden places.

Emily stepped out into the sunlight with pail in hand. She was heading for the spring to bring back water. Daddy was gone hunting and, strangely, her momma was still asleep, so Emily wanted to surprise her by having the chore all done before she got up. Strolling along the path through the wild flowers to the spring, Emily worried about her momma. She had seemed so tired lately and looked so pale.

As she moved toward the spring, Emily admired the wild flowers dotting either side of the path. The spring was one of her favorite places on the mountain. She loved kneeling in the cool grass and sipping water from the dipper fashioned from a gourd. The rippling and gurgling sounds of the water were soothing. Emily filled her pail and headed home, picking a few wildflowers for her momma as she went. She hoped the flowers would cheer momma up and make her smile.

Walking along, Emily noticed a yellow bird following her, flitting from branch to branch.

"I wonder why it isn't afraid of me?"

Moving to the cabin steps, Emily watched as the bird flew to the cherry tree, landing on a branch near the porch and peering at her as if it wanted something. As she opened the door, Emily looked for the bird one last time, but it was gone.

It dawned on Emily that her momma should be awake by now, rattling pots and pans as she prepared breakfast. But Momma was still in the bed; she had not moved at all since Emily had gone for water. Emily tried to place the flower in her momma's hand, but Momma did not move. Her hand felt cold.

"Momma! Momma!" Emily cried out. Over and over, but Grace did not move or answer the child's call.

Emily was afraid as she placed the flower in her mother's hand. She trembled as she sat there beside her momma, waiting for her daddy to come down from the higher mountains where he was hunting. Endless hours passed for Emily until finally her daddy walked through the door.

"Daddy! Daddy!" Emily cried. "Momma won't open her eyes. She won't talk to me!"

Malachi shook Grace gently, then more firmly as she failed to respond. Malachi stood, tears spilling from his eyes. His beloved Grace was gone.

Making his way to his straight-backed chair, Malachi reached for his daughter. "Come sit with Daddy, Emily." He lovingly drew his raven-haired child to him in a tight hug. Drawing back, he looked into his daughter's eyes. "Emily, honey, your momma is dead. Jesus wanted her to come to heaven and be a beautiful angel."

Emily stared into her daddy's eyes for a few seconds, then, without a sound, slid from his lap, ran out the door and across the porch heading in the direction of her favorite place in the woods. Lying down in the long grass of the meadow, Emily wept bitterly. She was filled with fear and uncertainty, unable to imagine life without her momma. Daddy had always been busy doing the work all men performed to provide for their families so Momma had been Emily's constant, the one guiding light in her life. She loved and respected her daddy, of course, but her bond with her momma was far more special and defining. In all her young life, she had never spent even an hour away from Momma. What would she do now?

Somehow Malachi found the strength to stand. He knew he should be doing something, but felt lost. Grace had been his rock, his guiding star. When things became too hard, one look at her or a kind word from her lips would sustain him. He knew he should go find Emily, but he did not want her to come back to the cabin until things were taken care of. He needed Nate and Ruth. Their steadfast friends, the first and best people they had met on Brush Mountain would help him do what needed to be done. With a last look at Grace where she lay so still on the bed, Malachi headed out the door and down the mountain.

Nate knew something was wrong the moment he saw Malachi coming down the trail. Calling for Ruth to come quickly, Nate got a closer look at his friend and felt a grip gather around his heart.

Walking into the yard, Malachi opened his mouth several times to speak, but his voice failed him. Finally he stammered out, "Grace is dead." He choked and continued, "I found Emily by her side this morning when I came back from hunting."

Laying a hand on Malachi's shoulder, Nate told his wife, "Let's go, Ruth. There are things that need to be done."

On their way to Malachi's cabin, they passed other homes, passing the word of what had occurred. Nate knew the news would travel fast, from house to house and beyond the mountain before very long. Nate knew that food would soon start appearing at the cabin, that men would come to help build the casket and carve the grave marker, and that - once Malachi decided where the grave should be - the ground would be opened to receive Grace into the mountains she loved so much.

While the men went into the barn, Malachi was not yet ready to see Grace again. For the few moments she knew she would have alone, Ruth laid her face in her hands and wept. Ruth had never had a friend like Grace. Her heart was broken and she knew she would never have another such friend. Grace had seemed so much a part of life on Brush Mountain it seemed wrong that she was no longer there.

As the neighbor ladies began to arrive, bearing burdens of food, cloth, and other necessary items for a burial, something mountain people were far too familiar with. Ruth's voice broke as she asked the ladies to help her wash Grace's beautiful dark hair. Together the ladies of the mountain worked to wash Grace's body and make her beautiful for her final rest. Ruth had brought a special, sweet-smelling soap Nate bought her for Christmas. Ruth was saving it for a special occasion, but could think of no more special purpose than to honor her friend one last time.

Choosing one of Grace's most beautiful, hand-sewn dresses, the ladies dressed their friend, combing her hair until it shone and arranging it as Grace had most liked it to be. The men were outside, fashioning a casket the women would line with the material they had brought, but for now Grace would lie on the feather bed she had made with her own hands, beneath a quilt she had sewn the previous winter. Ruth placed the flower Emily had picked for her mother beneath Grace's hand, knowing Grace would have wanted to hold her child's flower forever, just as she had hoped to hold her child.

Some of the women not present, Ruth knew, were cooking for the wake they would hold the next day. It was a tradition brought over from Scotland, handed down through generations upon generations of immigrant descendants who traveled into the Appalachian Mountains to make their home there. Neighbors were already gathering for the 'sitting up', the all night vigil for the dead.

Emily still lay in her field among the swaying, multi-colored flowers, unnoticed by the grief-stricken adults who had so much to do. She listened to the sound of the water, humming a soothing melody to herself, a song her momma loved to sing to her. Sometimes she drifted in and out of sleep, her emotions draining all her energy. She thought perhaps when she woke up she would find everything had just been a bad dream and her momma would be waiting in the yard, smiling to welcome her home.

Emily woke to the sight of the same yellow bird she had seen earlier that morning, perched on a redbud sprig. The bird made no sound at all, only sat watching Emily. For a moment, Emily felt a sweet peace flow through her, lifting her spirit. She realized her momma's death was as real as real could be. Suddenly the delicate little bird flew from the branch to light on Emily's knee. She reached out a trembling finger to lightly stroke the special bird. Tears fell from her eyes, blending with the rain just beginning to gently fall. The little bird flew away and the moment passed, but Emily seemed to remember that the older people said soft rain after someone died meant that person had made it to heaven. Surely, Emily knew, her momma was with Jesus now, just as Daddy had said.

Rising, Emily headed back toward the house. There were not that many people on Brush Mountain, but to see them all gathered on her porch was more than Emily could comprehend. Too many people when all she really wanted was to be alone. Slipping out of sight again, Emily headed for the rock chimney corner, a place that would forever be tainted by her sorrow.

Darkness was settling in when the rain stopped and Nate heard Emily's broken-hearted crying. Malachi had been out searching for her and Nate called to him before heading toward the rock chimney. The men had assumed the little girl was with the women, the women believed she was with the men so no one had missed the child until the work was nearly done. Malachi caught up to Nate and both rounded the rock formation partly hidden by a rose bush to find the little girl shivering in the near dark with tears streaming down her face.

Malachi went to his daughter, picking her up gently and carrying her to the house. Once inside, he sat Emily in a chair beside Grace.

Ruth promised, "I'll take care of her now and won't let her out of my sight."

Malachi nodded thanks.

Emily asked Ruth if she could sleep beside her momma. No one could deny her, it was as if the child knew this would be the last time she would ever be able to do so. The men gathered on the porch, served food by the women who stayed inside to be near their friend and her child. If Emily awakened confused or grieving, they would be there to help her.

When daylight came, Ruth was dozing in a chair beside the bed. A whimper from Emily brought her to alertness. She lifted the child carefully to her lap. Emily came slowly to full alertness, her face reflecting her inner struggle as she reviewed the events of the past day in her mind.

30

Ruth tried to explain what was going to happen next. "Emily, your momma is going to be put into that pretty box over there. Then she will go to heaven to be with Jesus and the beautiful angels."

Leading Emily to the table, Ruth encouraged her to eat a good breakfast. They had a long day ahead and would need their strength. Once the child finished, Ruth helped her bathe and change into one of the dresses her momma had made. Emily's clean dark hair was adorned with the little bows Grace always made to go with each dress.

Later in the morning, when everyone had eaten and prepared themselves as best they could, Grace was laid into her coffin and carried out beneath the oak tree she had loved so much. Malachi felt it would be a shelter for her in bad weather, shade for her in the summer, a final resting place where they could see her grave every day and, perhaps, she could watch over them.

Ruth sang as they walked, "Way back in the hills where Mother is sleeping, the angels took her to heaven one day, Mother's not dead, she's only a-sleeping..."

Emily seemed in shock, the full realization that she would never see her mother again sinking in.

Nate read from Psalms, "The mountains shall bring peace to the people, and the little hills, by righteousness. He shall come down like rain upon the mown grass; as showers that water the earth."

As Ruth led Emily away from the gravesite, Emily suddenly needed to be alone. She pulled on the hand holding hers and ran off to her secret place. Lying in the cool grass next to the bubbling stream, Emily looked up into the sky. The light rain which had been falling was now interspersed with sunbeams. Across the sky above the far ridge, a rainbow seemed to stretch forever. It was the most beautiful thing she had ever seen, the colors were so deep. She lay there a while and just absorbed the grandeur of the moment, the promise of the rainbow. Eventually the clouds moved on, obscuring the sun again, and the rainbow was gone. As the rain began to fall even harder, Emily felt like going home.

Everyone had left except for Nate and Ruth. Emily sat with Ruth a long time as the woman held her close. Finally, as dark came in earnest, they left too, and Emily and her daddy were alone. They sat staring into the fire as it died down in the grate, and said very little to one another. Emily kissed her daddy goodnight and climbed into the loft he had built for her the year before. Emily cried herself to sleep, waking on and off through the night wishing her momma was there to snuggle with once more. She realized anew that she would never again feel the warmth of her mother.

Chapter 5

The long grieving process seemed to last forever but eventually it was once again Emily's birthday. The year was 1884 and the little girl was six. Despite her youth, Emily was doing a woman's work. Carefree childhood days became a thing of the past as there always seemed to be chores to be done. Her momma had taught her well and Emily took on far more than a child her age should have been expected to do. Her daddy became more and more distant from her, seeming not to notice the burden he had placed on his daughter. Before Emily was seven, Malachi had remarried to a woman named Annie. Emily did not take well to her new stepmother and things got even worse when, just before Emily was eight, Annie had a child.

The older Emily got, the more neglected she felt. Her daddy, whom she had loved so much, was a stranger to her now. Emily had never felt so alone. She lived in constant fear of displeasing her father and step-mother.

Emily still sought refuge in her secret place when she could. She would go there every chance she got and hide away with her sorrow, but those moments of peace were all too few.

The sadness in Emily's heart never seemed to abate. It reflected back in it in the mirror every time she combed her long hair. She remembered how sad her momma's eyes could be at times and now understood that it was because Grace feared her happiness could not last. For Emily it was the knowledge that her life might never get any better. She was aware every moment that her life had irrevocably changed the morning her mother died.

Eventually Emily became old enough to blossom into womanhood, but she had no one to turn to for advice. In fear of what was happening to her, she ran into the mountains. There she found an isolated stream to wash her soiled clothes, then dried them on tree branches or rocks, often putting them back on still damp so she could return home before she got in trouble. By now her daddy and Annie had more children and Emily's burden grew even as the family increased. Emily wondered sometimes what may have happened if her mother had lived. What she would not have given to have her momma there to ask the many questions about life and her body that arose as she got older.

Emily struggled to please her father and step-mother, but never seemed to feel she fit in or was loved and accepted in the same way Annie's children were. She remembered the many bible stories her mother had told her as a child, but knew there was more than that to be learned.

The years slowly passed and Emily grew into a beautiful young woman. Each year that went by seemed only to highlight the emptiness she felt as she vainly sought to please her father.

One day, while picking berries in the meadow, a stranger came riding on a big, gray horse. He saw Emily and came to a sudden stop, watching her and trying to sit tall in his saddle to impress her. He seemed quite a bit older than Emily.

"Hello, girlie. What's your name?"

"Emily H-hensley," was her shy reply.

"Well, Emily, my name is Lewis Smith. You shore are a perty thang. How 'bout I come a-courtin' you sometime?"

Emily was so shocked she could not reply. She had never been approached by a man this way.

Lewis kept showing up from time to time wherever Emily was. One summer day, Lewis showed up at the cabin door. Malachi rose to meet the stranger.

"Well, mister, I have come a-calling on your girl. Can I take her for a walk?" Lewis hitched his horse to a tree in the yard.

Malachi was silent for a moment, staring out at the gray horse. "You certainly can."

Emily had been listening to the conversation and went into the small bedroom Malachi had built to expand the cabin when he remarried. Annie helped Emily dress and make herself presentable, which surprised Emily who figured the prospect of marrying her off was as much a motivation as anything else.

When Emily came out onto the porch, Lewis seemed stunned. Emily wore one of her momma's best dresses; tiny flowers of blue and yellow patterned the dress from the high neck down to the full skirt, tiny buttons adorned the back and several rows of green brick-a-brack highlighted the front.

As they stepped off the porch, Emily's petite size made Lewis seem taller than he really was. Lewis admired her shining hair, washed with rainwater and a special shampoo Ruth bought her for her sixteenth birthday. More than once he said she looked like an angel. Except for Ruth, who she hardly ever saw anymore, no one since her momma had called Emily beautiful or acted as if she were special; it was easy for her to believe Lewis.

"Emily, let's me and you walk out to that little place you love so well where all them wild flowers grow."

Emily took his hand and followed. She felt so good inside to think someone liked her.

"You shore look good, Emily."

She was unsure what to say so just smiled and said nothing.

The meadow was at the height of its beauty that mid-spring day, clothed in multicolored flowers and green grass, dogwoods and redbuds blooming. The water rippling past was the only sound for a time.

Finally, Lewis said, "This is the perfect time." He turned to look at her. "Will you marry me, Emily?"

He took her hand and kissed it gently. Emily blushed as she looked at Lewis, thinking how it would be to be married and able to get away from the terrible situation in her home. She remembered a time when Malachi had beaten her until she was sure she could take no more. Knowing he had done it to please his new wife had hurt all the more. She thought to herself, could this be any worse?

"Yes, I will."

Lewis led Emily to believe he could provide well for her. He told her that he already had a cabin over on the south side of Black Mountain overlooking Martin's Fork. 'Well, you can't see Martin's Fork from the cabin, but there's a path leading down to it."

Lewis smiled, but had no intention of treating Emily well. He believed she was a good worker and would obey her man. They walked back to the cabin where Lewis asked Malachi for permission to marry Emily.

"I'd be obliged if you married my girl," Malachi said.

Emily was not aware that the two men had known each other a long time before Lewis had ridden into her meadow. Annie had introduced them, certain marrying off her stepdaughter was the one sure way of getting rid of Emily, who looked far too much like Grace for Annie's comfort.

Annie helped Emily pack her things into a pillowcase her mother had made while Lewis unhitched his big gray horse and walked it alongside the porch. Emily handed over her clothes and climbed on, riding side-saddle behind Lewis. She locked her arms around him and they rode away. Emily asked Lewis to ride past her special place one last time. He guided the horse past the wild flowers and mountain springs, then turned them toward his home. Tears slid down Emily's face as she left her Camelot behind.

They rode down the mountain into Stone Mountain to the Britton Gap, going into Virginia to get their marriage license. A Justice of the Peace performed the ceremony and they headed back through the gap and down the trail to George Hensley Hollow. Following the trail up the hollow to the foot of Black Mountain, they were finally going up the path to Lewis' Place.

Emily looked upon the relatively level bench of the mountain, noting the one room cabin, and apple tree in bloom, and a natural spring running near the tree. The land was beautiful, but not as lovely as the home she had left on Brush Mountain. Emily saw the potential for good gardening, the land was in good shape and she felt she could make it even better. She grieved for her momma, and for her daddy as he had been before he married Annie. She knew this place was God's country too, but would never compare to the beauty of her Brush Mountain home. She knew the serenity of her home had been crafted in large part by her momma, but that serenity had been lost long ago. She visualized what she had known when Grace was alive and it pierced her heart to know it was irretrievably gone.

Black Mountain could hardly compare as neither tangible nor intangible things would be the same in her sixteen year old heart. She drew upon the inner strength she knew came from her momma and promised herself she would make her new life work no matter how high she had to reach spiritually, physically and emotionally.

After she took her belongings inside the cabin, she felt suddenly tearful.

"Lewis, I'll be back. I need to be alone for a while."

Her new husband seemed not to mind.

Emily walked around the bench of the mountain until she came to a brook winding its way down the mountain with a soothing trickle. She sat for what seemed like an eternity, thinking of the past, how much of her life echoed with the sound of flowing water. Finally she felt ready to go back to the cabin, telling herself that the past was gone. "Momma is gone, my life is now." As she headed back along the trail, Emily drew upon her inner strength. She was as solid as the mountain she stood on, it was her strength now.

Looking to the sky, she prayed, "I have a sadness in my heart, Lord, that tells me it will face a world of coldness, but Momma always said you would be with me and I believe her. Let the water flood overflow me, either let the deep swallow me up, and let not the pit shut her mouth on me. Blessed be the Lord God, the God of Israel, who only doeth wondrous things." Emily vaguely remembered the scriptures Grace had taught her and resolved in her heart to be a survivor.

Chapter 6

It was a fine spring morning and Lewis was up bright and early.

"Emily, I'll be back before dark, you have my supper cooked."

Lewis had told Emily that he worked down in Martin's Fork at the Government Distillery at a place he called the Old Red House near the river. He said he would never work in the mines as so many other men did. Emily had no idea what the Old Red House was or if someone lived in it. She wondered if it was a Road House, a place where she heard that men and women gathered to drink and do mean things.

After Lewis left for work, Emily felt well in her spirit, determined to make the best of her new situation. She worked hard to clean the dirty cabin. She scrubbed the split log floors with white sand she got from the basin of the spring. By the time the floor was dry, it was now a light gray. Emily had brought a few yards of yellow cloth that had belonged to Grace and some other things from her own sewing basket. She would get to sewing as soon as the cleaning was done.

She took the towels, dishcloths and bed covers to the stream and washed them with the washboard she found. She scrubbed them with lye soap she had brought along then hung them from a wire to dry. They were no match for her mother's many colored quilts, but by the time they dried they would be fresh with mountain air. While the laundry dried, she took her yellow cloth and sewed a set of curtains for the pair of small windows. She had enough string to run through the curtain headers to hang them. She put nails on each side of the window and tied off the string to hang the curtains, making a bow to tie them back on either side.

Once the bed linens dried, she brought them in and made the bed. She had found a table cloth in a trunk and washed that also. Once she put it on the scrubbed table top, the cabin started to look more homey. She cleaned the cook stove, lit a fire, and put supper on, proud of her days work. She was sure Lewis would be surprised and proud of her.

While supper simmered on the stove, Emily sat in the doorway looking over her new mountain home. She saw the same sort of bounty she had known on Brush Mountain; dogwoods and redbuds, lush green oaks, maples, and poplars. Hickory and black walnut trees spoke of a fall harvest of nuts to help them through the winter. She felt a peace come over her; her man had a good job, and things would be better than they had ever been at Brush Mountain after her momma died. She felt like a princess; she had bathed and washed her hair, put on a clean dress. She felt pretty and wanted.

Staring down the path, she knew she would see Lewis riding up any time.

"Life will be good," she said to herself. She imagined Lewis would want to take her over to Virginia on Saturdays to buy things she had never had before.

Suddenly she saw her man approaching on a big brown horse with a white face and stockings. She was sure he had bought the horse for her. Emily checked to make sure dinner was still warm, then stepped outside.

"Look what I brought you, Emily!"

Emily smiled in appreciation. She felt special for the first time in many years.

"Let's take him down to the barn, Emily. This is your horse, my wedding present to you." Emily's heart leapt with joy. She stroked the horse's side and he seemed to bond with her there and then.

Lewis told her to go put supper on the table while he fed the horses. "I have a lot to tell you," he said.

Emily went in and quickly put the meal on the table. She felt so hopeful. She thought to herself, I'm going to have a good life here. I'll garden, preserve food, keep a clean house, milk the cow and do everything I can for our home while Lewis makes a living with the Government.

Lewis walked in and patted her on the back, taking in everything she had accomplished. "Emily, you shore have made this place look real purty. Everything smells so fresh and clean. I knew you were a keeper when I first laid eyes on you."

"Are you ready for supper, Lewis?"

He nodded and walked to the small table where the wash water and basin sat. He washed up and joined Emily at the table she had made so pretty. Lewis looked at her strangely, but said nothing as he dished up his food and took a bite of fried ham.

"I have something to tell you, Emily. The Government Distillery is being moved out of Martin's Fork. Today was my last day. But I did work enough to buy a cow, some chickens, a couple of pigs, a bull tongue plow, some seed, and a couple of hoes. That's about all a man needs if he has a good help mate. After I met you, I started buying all this stuff. The cabin didn't cost too much to build; a couple of men from the distillery helped me with it. It's been a purty good year, I guess."

Emily began to feel uneasy, it sounded as if Lewis had no plans for getting a new job.

"I can make moonshine again," he said. "I've done it before and I can do it again."

Emily nearly choked on her food. She had nothing to say; only negative thoughts occupied her mind at this news.

The Lewis Place on Black Mountain (after mountain top removal)

Britton Gap

The Government Distillery - Lewis is the one holding the shovel

Chapter 7

Come planting time, Emily knew the signs that helped discern when which vegetables were likely to grow best. The spring passed into summer as Emily worked steadily raising food and preserving it for winter. Lewis helped very little.

Autumn came on, stirring hope in Emily's heart as the beautiful foliage made the mountains seem on fire. Winter, however, brought a stark reality. Emily felt as if she were waking from a long dream only to realize what she had been living was the dream. She became aware of a loss of strength, sapping the good health she had always enjoyed. When the morning sickness came, she was excited but circumstances put a damper on her elation. She waited a few weeks before sharing the news with Lewis. She hoped he would be excited and help her more with the chores, but he showed no emotion at all. Emily began to realize she was not appreciated at all except for the work she could perform. Her dreams of a better life dwindled away, but she had no one to turn to and no where to go.

Emily gave birth to her baby in early spring, by mid-spring she was out on the mountain clearing new ground to grow more food for their expanded family. She knew they could not survive if she did not put the work into preparing, growing, and harvesting the food to sustain them. Once planting was done, Emily talked Lewis into helping her build another room onto their cabin for the new baby and future children they were likely to have. She worked as hard as any man, and certainly harder than her husband. Along with tending her garden, Emily took care of the milk cow, the pigs, and the chickens, knowing the livestock was an integral part of their survival. She had developed into a strong willed mountain woman, someone who did not accept her circumstances but fought to improve them.

She realized there were other needs she could neither build nor grow. She lay awake at night worrying about how to get essentials like flour, salt, sugar, and yard goods to clothe her children. It came to her that she could raise extra food then carry it through Britton Gap to Rose Hill, Virginia. There she could trade for what they needed and get her corn ground into meal for cornbread. Emily had another child but never slowed down. She took only a few days to rest after childbirth, then got back to work to support her family.

One bitter winter, filled with blizzards and frigid temperatures, Emily rose at dawn and saddled her horse. She headed down the mountain path, chilled to the bone already, heading toward Britton Gap. She needed Vick's Salve, among other things, for when the children suffered chest colds and congestion. To her, Vicks was the cure-all for almost any ailment. She made it to Virginia and accomplished her trades, but the temperature was dropping by the hour. Every mile she traveled seemed colder than the last. After crossing the gap and the Martin's Fork River, literally frozen over, Emily finally made it to the mountain, she could see the streams were frozen solid. She began to shake as the cold, cold wind seemed to find every hole and seam in her clothing. Prince, her horse, was a fine, strong animal, but he began to slow down as they climbed. Even he was chilled to the bone.

Prince moved up the hollow to the foot of Black Mountain, following the trail on instinct. Snow and dusky sunset made it impossible to see. Emily could tell Prince was afraid, usually he would quicken his pace as they got nearer to home, but this time he plodded carefully.

It was almost dark when they reached the cabin. As Emily attempted to dismount, she realized she was literally frozen to the saddle. She refused to panic, she had too much spunk to let something like this get the better of her. She pulled her clothes from the saddle as they ripped and crackled with ice. She soothed Prince and led him to the barn, covering him with a quilt to ward off the chill now that he was no longer moving. It took every bit of energy she had left to carry her goods into the house. Not unexpectedly, Lewis did not rush to greet her.

Looking into the eyes of her children, Emily realized her arduous journey had been more than worth the danger. She knew she would be able to meet their needs for at least a few more weeks. On all her trading trips, Emily always managed to get a stick of peppermint candy for each child. The look of gratitude and the smiles on their faces warmed her heart, but could not ease the chill in her worn body.

Britton Graveyard

How Emily may have looked riding through the gap
(picture is her great granddaughter Kimberly Harber)

Chapter 8

One cold, treacherous winter, Emily's firstborn daughter Josie came down with whooping cough. Josie was five years old, the spitting image of her mother. Emily knew only old-time doctoring and remedies. She did everything in her power to save her baby, but beautiful little Josie died in her mother's loving arms. Emily's soul was crushed, but she knew she had to carry on for the sake of her remaining two children. She buried her little Josie in Britton graveyard near Britton Gap. She stopped by the grave many times on her trips through the gap to trade. Emily felt as if part of her soul had died the day she laid her child in the ground. She never spoke of it to anyone until she was much older.

Despite the hard work and harder times, Emily had grown into a beautiful woman. She had the same Cherokee beauty of her mother and blue eyes made the more striking by her dark complexion. She was small, but very strong. She plowed fields, and cleared ground for new planting. She could cut trees with a double-bladed axe and chop the trees into firewood to see them through winter. There were times in the winter when water would drip from her dress tail to form icicles.

Lewis would lay warm by the fire kept going by Emily's hard work. He would nip at his 'shine' but watched the children well enough. He knew Emily would make him pay one way or the other if he failed. The children were trained to go to bed very early.

One particular evening while chopping firewood, Emily felt more angry than usual. The more she chopped, the angrier she became. Eventually she felt like a volcano ready to erupt. Her very heart and soul cried out so loudly she was sure they could hear it across the mountains in Virginia. But she held her emotions inside. As she began to slide large pieces of logs down the hill to where she chopped wood, she felt provoked into doing something.

"I'll fix that sorry dog," she muttered to herself. "Just let him be sleeping in front of the fire, the logs I've cut popping and cracking as he snores. I'll fix that devil."

Just as darkness eased its way into Black Mountain. Emily walked to the edge of the ridge base high on the mountain above the house. Making her way to the woodshed, petite little Emily held a debate with herself. "Should I, or shouldn't I?"

Suddenly she headed across the yard. She could feel her temper rising with every step. In no time she was at the door, swinging the heavy wooden thing open in one push. There he lay in front of the fireplace just as she had known he would be.

'Don't look like no prince to me,' she thought to herself. 'I'll fix him…'

Her insides were already hot enough. Emily stood in front of the fire, warming her hands. She had delicate work to do.

Emily moved quietly to the corner of the room where her sewing basket set out on the old chest. She opened the box and drew out her longest needle and strongest thread. After threading the needle, she closed the door to the room where her children slept. She did not want them to awaken while she put her plan in motion. Quietly, she drew a sheet from the quilt stack she kept in the corner of the room opposite the kitchen area. The fire flared, giving her light enough to carry out the unkind courtesy she was about to perform upon her sleeping prince. Lewis was so drunk from his new run of shine he barely groaned as she rolled him over onto the sheet. Pulling each side to the middle of his body, Emily began to sew. She found herself grinning until Lewis groaned a little. She started sewing faster thinking, 'This will give you something to remember.'

When Emily was finished, she peeked in on the children to be sure they were soundly asleep before moving to the next step in her plan. She eased back to where her Prince Charming lay; pulling a little at the seams she had made to assure herself they were strong. Lewis sighed, comfortable in his sheet cocoon. Emily stepped quietly to the corner where her broom hanged on a nail. It was a good, strong broom she had made herself from a locust sapling. The straw scratched a little as she turned that end toward her own body and got a good grip below the wire that held the straw to the handle. Positioning the broom, she smiled a little, but it was still an angry smile. The closer she got to Lewis the more outraged she became. Her mind was crowded with all the injustices she and her children had endured thanks to this man. As she drew nearer, the fire flared up again, highlighting perfectly her sorry no-account man.

"He'll long remember this…"

She was still a moment, she would never know if it was second thoughts staying her hand or something else, but her arms and hands seemed to coil with the anger she had held so long and she drew back the broomstick, drawing it down on his body. She hit his head, his arms, anything that was in her path with all the strength she could muster.

Lewis jerked and squirmed and kicked trying to escape the sheet.

"You sorry, no good, piece of a man. Can you feel this? Let's see how good you sleep now!"

She beat him until her anger abated, and she felt he had enough. She didn't want to go to jail. The thought crossed her mind that she had best not beat him to death.

By the time she finished, Lewis was almost under the bed. She was unsure if he had passed out from the shine or if she had rendered him unconscious. She lay her hand on his chest and felt a strong heartbeat, so she knew he was alive.

She pulled the number two washtub down from the wall and filled it with warm water from the reservoir in the cook stove. She took a bath and rinsed from a jug of water she had placed on the floor by the tub. Stepping out, she dried herself and dressed in a warm flannel gown. She went to the stove and broke off a piece of cornbread, dipped out a serving of potatoes and pork, and cut a little onion into it. Going back to her fire, she sat and ate like the delicate mountain princess she had once believed she would be.

Emily left Lewis under the bed all night and had the best night's sleep she could remember for some time. She had unleashed a mountain of frustration she had held inside for years and the utter relief she felt sent her into a deep rest her body had needed so long.

Sometime in the night, the shine wore off and Lewis became chilled. He wiggled and squirmed his way out of the sheet. He was sober now, but could not remember exactly how he came to be in the

49

state he found himself in. Lewis was not sure if his nightmares had come true and it had been Emily who did this to him or if a wild animal had paid him a ruthless visit.

Chapter 9

Emily struggled hard bringing up her children: John, Fannie, Steve, Liddie, Roosevelt, and Bair. She had another child, Ruthie, who would come along later.

She gave birth to one of her children alone in the log cabin; no one was within miles that day. Her floor was clean, as always scrubbed with white sand from the still pools of the spring. As she realized she was in hard labor, Emily boiled water to sterilize scissors and laid out a clean white sheet she had been careful not to wash in lye soap; she did not want anything harsh to touch the delicate skin of her baby. She cut a piece of sterile white linen to tie off the navel cord.

Emily laid the white sheet on the floor when the time came. The little one was born finally. Cutting the cord and tying it off, she bathed her new baby and wrapped it in a baby-sized quilt she had made. After tending to her personal needs, Emily relaxed in bed with her new baby. As always, Emily continued to be a survivor for her children all her life; she never truly got over losing her little Josie.

One late October day, Emily rode her horse up to Britton Gap to visit Josie's grave. As she knelt on the cool ground, tears ran in a steady stream down her face. The roses she had planted still bore a few yellow blooms and she brought one to place on her baby's grave. She finally stood in silence, staring at the name carved on the river rock that served as Josie's headstone. She climbed on her horse and started away, looking back only once before riding away. The autumn breeze dried her tears as she headed on into Britton Gap and her business of keeping her family fed.

She worried as she rode about the children at home. With winter coming, they all had need of warm winter clothes, shoes, and coats.

When she arrived in Virginia, Emily unloaded her heavy sacks of fall beans. While trading for her needed goods, she could not stop herself from touching the cloth she knew would make perfect warm clothes, and the shoes on the shelves were perfect. But they were far too expensive and she knew her wishes were useless.

Emily packed her flour, meal, and other necessities on Prince and turned him back toward home. She stopped partway there, just enjoying the colors of fall, the crimsons and golds warming her heart. Near the top of the mountain, the sun had faded. Stopping to hobble Prince's feet before descending, Emily saw a man ride out of the shadow of the trees. Sometimes she felt she was being watched as she rode, but she had never encountered anyone on her ride before.

She had no way of knowing at the time, but the man had enquired about her. He knew her dire circumstances and had even seen her staring sadly in the store at things she needed but could never afford.

"Emily," he said in a low voice.

His voice in the silent woods startled her. "Who are you and why have you been watching me?"

The man was a smooth talker but not bad looking. He was also very confident in himself.

"Let's talk for a while, you look a little tired."

Emily was always in a hurry, rarely noticing or taking time to look down into the valley to admire the beauty there. She saw only trees and the path to and from home. All she thought of was getting home to her children.

For some reason, Emily pondered his request this day. "I guess I have a little time."

The man extended his hand and led her to the edge of the ridge. As they walked, the man propositioned her, quoting a sum. He knew how desperate she was for money. She could not help but think she could clothe her children well for the winter with that kind of money. Her mind was filled with fear and guilt; fear of what she was going to do to keep her children warm through the winter, and guilt that she was even considering his offer.

Emily felt guilty to her dying day.

Emily's son, John, his wife, Maudie, and their son Ambrose Smith

Ambrose and wife, Cora. Second row: Beulah, Shirley, Claudetta, Mikey. Back row: Ricky, Jim, Dennis, Justin Monroe, Johnny.

Emily's son, Steve's children - Alberta, Kelly, and Clifford

Hazel. Louannie, Steve, and Claude

Kelly's wife, Mary; Louannie and daughter Alberta (1950s)

Steve's son, Clifford Smith (1950s)

Chapter 10

Much later, Emily gave birth to her last child. Ruthie was a special child, full of a goodness that stayed with her throughout her life. As soon as she was old enough, Ruthie wanted to walk off the mountain to church and accepted Jesus into her heart at the age of seventeen.

As her children became old enough, they moved off the mountain. Roosevelt and Liddie ended up in Catron's Creek. Fannie, Bair, Steve, and Ruthie moved on the opposite side of the mountain into Martin's Fork.

Emily and Lewis remained in their little log cabin on Black Mountain. Emily did not have to work as hard in later years, but it was lonely with her children gone. Emily and Lewis favored Martin's Fork, a valley snuggled in the corners formed by Black Mountain, Brush Mountain, and Stone Mountain. Martin's Fork was an untouched treasure. The mountains hovered over the valley, shining in rich tones in the spring and fall. Dogwood, sarvis, and redbuds dotted the landscape in the spring. Some lived on mountains and ridges, while others settled into the valley. Children would gather walnuts, hickory nuts, and hazelnuts from trees that were never planted by human hands. Cardinals, bluebirds, orioles, and many other birds sang tunes that spoke to the soul of the people who lived there. The mountains clothed the people with abundant sunshine, fresh air and pure water. While they possessed few material things, they were rich in ways many in large cities could never appreciate.

Only a few people remained in the high mountains. Ruthie's first cousin from Malachi's second marriage, Clara Hensley, was one such lady. She had to walk off the ridge to a low-lying stream to carry water. This had been a hardship for her for many years. One day she experienced a miracle with her own eyes.

A huge oak tree stood only a short distance from her house. As she walked in her yard she heard the gurgling of water. She stopped, listening intensely. Following the sound, she realized it came from the tall oak tree. Drawing near, she saw clear water bubbling from beneath the roots. She ran to the shed and got tools. She dug a spring that very day that never went dry. Clara was finally able to build a spring house to keep her milk and butter cold. In later years, Clara moved down into the valley into George's Hollow. She had a little house snuggled at the base of Black Mountain.

Ruthie had not married yet by this time, but stayed with relatives in Martin's Fork. Ruthie never minded hard work. Ruthie had only ever had hand me down coats, but with wages from her work she would now be able to buy her first new coat.

When her brother Steve and his wife had their first child, Ruthie stayed with them to help. Steve had a car and took Ruthie on her first car ride out of Martin's Fork into Harlan.

As they chugged through Martin's Fork, crossing in and out of the shallow river at times on the dirt highway, Ruthie looked around at Steve occasionally to see his humble smile. Knowing her brother was all too familiar with this new part of life made her feel more comfortable.

"How much further, brother? Seems to me like we're a long way from home."

Steve loved being the first to show his young sister a whole different world. Ruthie's eyes danced with excitement.

When Steve parked his car, he said, "Come on, Ruthie. I'll take you to a dry good store."

As they walked, Ruthie felt like she was in a foreign land. This was so different from the mountains and valley she had always known. Timidly, she walked into the store behind her brother.

"The women's clothes are over there, Ruthie."

Nervously, Ruthie walked over to the ready-made dresses. She could hardly wait to touch the soft crepe material. Never in her life had she owned anything but homemade clothes. Her eyes suddenly lit upon a brown crepe dress with a cream colored Victorian lace collar. Taking the dress off the rack, she held it up against her slim body, trying to determine if it would fit. Deep inside, she felt a little guilty. This was too nice, it was more than she deserved. Holding on to the dress, she moved toward the coats. She was full of anticipation, aware her brother watched from a distance with a big grin on his face. Laying the dress across the rack, Ruthie pulled one off it's hanger and tried it on. It was a perfect fit. After a moment, she took the coat off, replaced it on the hanger, and lay it beside the dress. Examining the prices, Ruthie hoped she would be able to afford both. To her surprise, she had more than enough. Over near the wall, Ruthie saw a selection of shoes. The coat and dress were brown so she looked at the brown leather ones, choosing a somewhat dressy pair with a stack heel.

Ruthie smiled at her brother and, after paying for her goods, she and Steve set out to fill Louannie's grocery list.

Bouncing along the road back home, Ruthie could hardly wait to get back home to the bedroom with the wardrobe mirror. She held her packages tight as they forded the river, she did not want her new things getting wet where the water was deep enough to come up over the running boards of the car.

Come Sunday morning, she knew she would look like a princess in her new finery as she walked to church.

That very Sunday she met a man on the path near the cliff hole, so named for the water hole nestled among the steep cliffs there. As they met on the path, their eyes locked. It was love at first sight.

The man shyly bid her hello and tipped his hat and she continued on to the one-room school house that also served as a church. After services, when she walked outside, the tall, handsome man was waiting.

"Can I walk you home?"

"I guess so."

They only spoke a little as they walked, but wedding bells were ringing in both their heads.

Henry had been working in the mines several years already. He lived with his grandparents, George and Ada Hamlin, and had since he was a boy. Henry was older than Ruthie by a few years and was ready to settle down.

One lovely day as he waited for Ruthie just below the church, his mind was made up. Beautiful Ruthie came from the church following her usual path. Henry waited, leaning against a huge maple until she came to where he stood then fell into step beside her. He eased his hand in to cover hers and softly said, "Ruthie, will you marry me?"

They walked around the cliff hole path high above the river. Ruthie was flattered beyond words and waited until they reached level ground before stopping to check her shoes and dress for debris. Slowly she raised her head, her brown eyes looking deeply into his apprehensive blue ones. Ruthie reached up to touch his shoulders and said, "Yes, Henry, I will marry you."

Henry heard joyful sounds in his head as he touched her pretty face. She was everything he had ever wanted.

Not long after, Ruthie wore her beautiful brown crepe dress with the lace collar for the second time at her wedding.

They had to go into Brush Mountain to the nearest ordained preacher. Ruthie's nephew, Fannie's son George Hamlin, went with them as a witness. Ruthie rode sidesaddle on a horse while the men walked alongside. She was pretty as a picture to Henry's eyes. Once the ceremony was over, they headed back to Martin's Fork, stopping off to pick up Ruthie's belongings before heading for their new home on the plot of land Henry had bought. His uncle, Big John Hensley, had helped him build the little house. Henry had bought enough furniture to accommodate them in the beginning: a table, bed, stove and a few chairs. It was a good start, and soon more furniture followed as Henry worked and brought home his pay.

Ruthie was happy as a humming bird. She loved her little house; it was home. Golden seal linoleum covered all the tongue and groove floors except for the threshold between rooms which she painted brown. The Victorian posts and banisters and clapboard siding she painted white.

Some time later, Big John, single and on his own, came by and approached his nephew and new niece with an offer. "Can I board with you? I will pay you well."

Henry kindly replied, "Indeed you can."

They were a family. Henry's father had died a few days before he was born, as a result, Henry had always had a special connection to Big John, his dad's brother.

While the men worked, Ruthie busied herself with keeping the house and cooking; her sweet nature set a pleasant atmosphere for the home.

Ruthie was out working in her yard one day and saw a wild hog browsing around on the hill, rooting the ground for food. She eased up quietly and saw the hog go into her barn. She moved quickly and quietly to slam the door closed thinking her husband, Henry, would be proud of her for capturing the hog. It would mean fresh pork for their family for the winter. Henry worked across the mountain at the Black Star mines. As he had to walk the mountain, she knew it would be dark but the next day was Saturday and he would not have to go to work.

Ruthie knew Big John would help Henry kill the hog. The next day the men did exactly that, cutting the hog's throat then hanging it from poles to bleed out. Boiling hot water was used to scald the hair off the hide, any remaining hair was scraped off with a sharp knife. Once the hair was removed, the hog was cut from throat to stomach, and the organs were removed. The meat was then cut into hams, shoulders, bacon, ribs and pork chops. The meat was salted, then stored in the smoke house either hung from the ceiling or stored on board shelves. Big John handed off some fresh pork chops for frying and Ruthie was proud to cook them. She was so excited to know she had captured this meat herself. She stood over the cast iron skillet as the pork chops sizzled. She smiled as she scurried around her kitchen, dipping shuck beans out of the huge pot into a big bowl and placing them on the her green checked tablecloth. Cornbread was flipped onto a plate out of a cast iron skillet; Ruthie smiled to see it was a perfect golden brown. She stood over the pork chops with her fork in hand, ready to take them up when they were perfectly cooked. Once they were cooked to perfection, Ruthie called out the back door to the men.

"Dinner's ready!!"

The three of them sat down to eat the meal Ruthie was so proud of. They gave thanks for the meal and began to fill their plates. Big John was the first to bite into the fresh brown pork chops. Ruthie sat waiting for some sound of praise, but one look at John's face told both Ruthie and Henry something was wrong.. They both tasted their own chops and realized immediately why John was acting so strangely. They realized then that wild pork had a strong, nasty taste and was as tough as old shoe leather.

Ruthie felt like crawling under the table, but Big John and Henry laughed and laughed even though they had labored all day over that wild hog. Ruthie felt a little better, thanks to the men's good sense of humor, but she was thinking that old boar had caused them a day of work for nothing. From then on she would only raise 'tame hogs' as she thought of the piglets in her pen.

Ruthie loved Martin's Fork valley far more than Black Mountain. She could stand in her yard and stare up at the mountain and think of old times, the memories it held both pleasant and unpleasant.

Within a few years, Ruthie gave birth to her son, Rodney, and in 1940, her daughter Pauline (called Paulie). Three others would follow.

Ruthie and Paulie 1941

Rodney and Harold

Ruthie and Morine

Wilhelmina 1959

Henry, Grandparents Ada and George Hamlin

Henry Hensley

Chapter 11

In Martin's Fork, milk cows roamed the hills moving down to the low grassy areas until they heard voices echoing in the cool of the evening. "Sook Hef! Sook Hef!" The children hunted the cows; their faces lighting with joy when they heard the bells hung around the cow's necks. When the cows came home, the mothers would milk them sitting on a bucket not useful for anything else, or squatting if there was no bucket. Most did not have the luxury of a stool. The milk played a melodious tune as first one hand then the other expressed the milk into the shiny metal buckets.

As a child in the forties, Paulie would sit behind Momma Ruthie as she expertly filled her milk bucket using both hands. The sound would forever ring in her ears when she remembered those wonderful days.

One evening at milking time, Paulie felt as if she and her momma were in a desolate place. Standing behind her tall, beautiful, dark-haired mother, Paulie could hear the sound of the water rippling in the stream nearby. Paulie was barely ten years old, but felt ready to weep as she looked into the sky.

"Momma, why is the sky so red?"

"Honey, that is a sign there is a war away across the waters. Our boys from America are fighting to protect us."

Paulie just stood there for the longest time, staring into the amber sky as she tried to figure out why this had to be. Paulie was so small but understood young men were dying somewhere so she could be safe to roam the mountains and streams safely.

Somewhere in time, Ruthie's mother Emily or someone else in the family had discerned the skies and connected them to what was taking place in the world at the time. With very little communication with the world outside their mountains and valleys, people were left to feel in their spirits if all was well or not.

One sad day Ruthie's sister, Fannie, who lived across the river at the base of Stone Mountain, received news that her son, Lewis Hamlin, had been wounded in the war. Paulie had never experienced such emptiness and sadness as she did watching their sad faces. As their tears fell, Paulie's chest tightened and she felt all choked up. Being so young, she could not comprehend everything, but sensed it was a time of sorrow. Thankfully, Lewis recovered and received multiple medals for his service, but it was a very trying time for Fannie as she waited for news.

Ruthie and Fannie always shared their sorrows as well as their joys. Fannie was a strong woman; she had already lost her husband and another of her sons, Edward, to tuberculosis. He left behind his beautiful wife, Viola, and their little girl, Shirley. Her boys - George, Clinton, Elmer, Edward, and Lewis - were only small boys when their father, Calvin, died and was buried in the Britton Graveyard. Fannie had to work hard to raise her children alone. She hoed corn for people and washed laundry by hand for fifty cents a day.

Ruthie once said that Fannie would give a full day's work for her pay. If she finished early, she would mop the floor or do some other chore until her time was up. Times were hard in the 1930s and she knew she was blessed to find work at all. Henry and Floyd loved Fannie and her children and helped out all they could.

Fannie's children never forgot watching their mother work so hard to take care of them. Every paycheck they earned was treasured and they made sure to take care of their mother.

Fannie's sons Edward and George, Ruthie's son, Rodney, in the middle. Edward died young of tuberculosis

Edward's daughter, Shirley

George Hamlin

Elmer Hamlin

Lewis Hamlin during Korean War

Lewis' medals after being wounded and missing in action

Clinton Hamlin

Sid Austin, Lewis Hamlin, Fannie Hamlin

Chapter 12

Up and down Martin's Fork valley in the 1930s and 1940s, women and children worked the gardens and fields after their men left to work the mines. The men left before daylight, their carbide lights attached to their hard mining caps to light their way to work. In the short days of the winter months, these men rarely saw daylight since they arrived at work before dawn and returned home after dark. No one was wealthy, very few were able to save money. Some of the men would take potato peelings for their work meals, leaving the potatoes for their families.

There was no welfare system back in those days. The community looked after one another. Neighbor helped neighbor. When one suffered hardships, others hurt for them and reached out to help. When one experienced a success, nearly all rejoiced for them.

No part of the world has ever been a true utopia, but for the most part the people of Martin's Fork possessed the unique spirit of caring for one another.

It has been said again and again that Floyd Hamlin was the best hearted man to ever hit Martin's Fork. Floyd was a sinner who had never taken part in church, but he found God in his old age. Many chose the church as their refuge as well as their social life, while others chose the 'devil's ways'.

Men would congregate near a natural spring beneath an oak tree near the mouth of George Hollow or near the river under a big hemlock tree. The men would play dice and drink moonshine. Sometimes men were shot as the moonshine would fuel their tempers. Sadly, it was not unusual for a few of these men to get drunk on 'shine and go home to beat their wives. Many times the men would be forgiven and the women would carry on with their lives fighting for survival.

One evening, just after Henry had begun boarding away from home in order to work in the Leatherwood mines for Blue Diamond coal, Ruthie, Rodney, Harold, Morine, and Paulie were home alone.

Down the dirt road just below the house, they could hear Joe beating Willa. The sound of that man's hands striking that pitiful young woman made Ruthie's blood boil.

"Children, you stay right here on the porch!"

Without pausing to put on shoes, Ruthie marched off the porch and ran barefooted down the dirt road. She grabbed the drunken man and yelled, "You take your rotten hands off her!"

Joe made no attempt to fight Ruthie. She took Willa to safety and let the drunken Joe find his way home.

Henry had never laid a hand on Ruthie so she could not abide such behavior. There was another night when she heard a neighbor in the cabin she and Henry rented out. Josh was drunker than a skunk that had raided a moonshine still. When Ruthie heard Josh beating his wife, Jill, she ran out her kitchen door, across the creek, and up the hill. The closer she got, the madder she got.

"Josh! You take your hands off Jill right now or I'll give you a taste of your own medicine!"

"This is my woman!" he shouted back, grabbing Jill and pulling her close to him.

"Then treat her like she's your woman and not some wild animal."

One night when Henry and Josh were away at work, Jill was visiting Ruthie's house. They could hear someone on the hill above the house under the tall oak that cast a shadow in the moonlight. Ruthie wanted to know where the noise was coming from. The window on that side of the house was open.

"Jill, children, stay right still while I get my forty-five pistol. I'll put whoever it is on their way."

She cocked the pistol and stuck her hands and arms out the window, aiming at the big oak then fired off a couple shots. It was scary for the children, but Ruthie was cool. The intruder fled. Years later it was told that the man was shot in the big toe but kept it a secret for a long, long time. The story was that he was trying to sneak to Josh and Jill's house to try his luck at getting involved in a relationship with Jill. Who knows?

On another occasion, Ruthie heard her chickens cutting a shine in their roost. She grabbed her forty-five automatic and ran out to protect her chickens. She heard years later that it was a man visiting the honky tonk house a ways down the road. He had agreed to steal a couple of chickens for a midnight snack for the gang. The story told is that he got no chickens, had hidden under the house until she went back inside, then ran away. Ruthie nipped their plan in the bud that night.

Chapter 13

For many years no one left Martin's Fork going north, south, or west to work in factories or other industries. They made moonshine, worked the mines, or cut trees. They lived on their own resources and ingenuity.

Old men who were strangers came into the valley. They could have come by way of the mountains or by some luck caught a ride into the beautiful mountains. Old Andy Smith and Sherman Clawnager were two who commonly stood in the doorway with only a small bag of clothes. Ruthie, Lottie Hensley, Harvey Wilson, Fannie, Floyd, and Wick Hamlin, among others, gave them a bed and food for days. Old Man Sherman would bring in firewood for his keep, at least he was unwilling to just take a chair and his comfort while others worked.

Sherman lived his life in that way for years, but was found dead one day in a natural spring in the mountains. Talk spread through the valley that old Sherman Clawnager likely bent down to get a cold drink of water, had a heart attack, pitched in headfirst and drowned.

Ruthie got the surprise of her life one summer day. The bees buzzing around the bee gums on the hillside above the stream were making honey for Ruthie and her family. The birds were singing, fresh water rippled down the hollow right past the kitchen window. Ruthie was in her glory, contentedly cooking dinner. She smiled as she worked; standing tall in her pretty floral cotton dress she had sewn herself. Her hair was done up in her usual fashion, tucked around a soft tube of fabric that circled her head. She bustled around the kitchen as she hummed 'Gathering flowers for the Master's Bouquet'.

As she turned her fried green tomatoes, she caught a glimpse of someone through the screen door. She turned to get a closer look and saw a tall, thin elderly man with gray hair and a beard. Looking into his ebony eyes, she was sure she had never met the man before.

"What brings you to these parts?" she asked.

The man stood in silence a moment, looking uneasy. "Well…I'm your daddy."

Ruthie sank into the straight back chair at the end of the kitchen table. She folded her arms on the table and laid her face on them. After a moment, she raised her head again to look upon this stranger.

"My daddy?" She was in shock. "Why did you wait thirty-two years to come my way?"

In her mind she was in turmoil. His claim could not be true. Lewis Smith was her daddy. If he was right, why had no one told her?

"Can I come in?" he mumbled. "I'm awful tired from my journey here."

"I guess." Ruthie was thinking to herself that she had no choice if she wanted to find out the truth of things.

The screen door whined as he opened it, the taut spring that kept it closed nearly caught him in the backside as he entered and let it go.

Ruthie suddenly remembered her dinner and jumped up to rescue the fried-green tomatoes and other dishes just in time. As she finished the meal and removed the food from the heat, she kept glancing over her shoulder at the man. He looked pretty shabby, she felt a little sorry for him and asked him if he wanted to eat.

"Yeah, I am awful hungry."

Ruthie went out on the kitchen porch and washed some cucumbers, onions and red tomatoes. She sliced them up and put them on the table with the cooked food.

The man just watched her, he seemed like he was starving. Ruthie finished setting the table and the man filled his plate, wolfing down his dinner as if he would never eat again.

Ruthie had no appetite, picking at the food she had spent hours preparing. Before long her children, who were out hoeing corn, would file in ready to eat. What would she tell them about this man sitting in their daddy's seat at the head of the table?

Finally the man finished eating and raised his head. "Looks to me like you need some help," he said. "I hear you have nine young'uns; four of yours and five of your sister Liddie's. Appears to me you need some help."

Ruthie's sister Liddie had passed away the previous December and her children had come to live with Ruthie and her family. Henry was working over in Leatherwood, too far to walk every day so he boarded with Dollie and Shorty Caldwell through the week and was only home on the weekends. Their family needed money and Henry had to go where the work was, but it left a lot of work on Ruthie. The man, who introduced himself as Charlie, had definitely done his homework. He knew she and the kids had to go to the stream to do their laundry, hauling the dirty clothes down to the water and heating it in big tubs, scrubbing things by hand on an old washboard, then rinsing in the stream. It was hard work, she had to admit it, but the children seemed to love it, especially when she would sing to them. She had to admit, also, that it was not as enjoyable an experience in the winter.

Charlie said persuasively, "You know, Ruthie, they make gasoline washing machines now."

Electricity had yet to come to Martin's Fork, so a gasoline washer would be something that could make their lives just a little bit easier. Ruthie thought of how she could set the washer on the porch of the little house on the hill that Big John had built not long before he died. The six boys slept there now and it was where she did her food preserving.

"With all these children, you sure could use a gasoline washing machine," he said again. "I tell you what, I'm going to buy you one!"

"Well, I could use one, sure. Wash day when the children are in school is hard on me."

Ruthie knew by now she would not be able to turn Charlie away whether he bought her a washer or not. She had been taking in elderly homeless people for years.

"That settles it then. I'll have you a washer here before the week is out. 'Pon my honor, I will."

Ruthie was nervous as she heard the children coming in from the fields, stopping to wash their hands at the old basin outside before filing through the door.

All nine children gathered around the table and sat down in their assigned seats, plainly curious about the stranger in their house. Ruthie could see they were not going to eat until the mystery at their table was solved.

Finally Ruthie spoke. "Children, this is Charlie Spurlock. Charlie, this is Rodney, Frank, Sam, Willard, Esco, Mary Ruth, Harold, Paulie, and Morine." Charlie tells me he's my daddy."

The children giggled nervously, thinking this must be some kind of joke. They had a grandpa already and that was Lewis Smith. They had no idea of how lazy the man had been or how hard Grandma Emily had struggled. To them, he was special.

"Mind your manners, children. Charlie will be staying with us for a few days."

As the children served themselves and ate their dinner, Ruthie could not help but think if Charlie was her father this visit would surely not be a one time thing. And indeed, it was not.

The gasoline powered washer came that week, as Charlie had promised, and the children were amazed. Charlie came and went, appearing from the foot of the mountain at regular intervals. Ruthie would see him coming through the white porch rails and call out to the children, "Here comes old Charlie."

She never loved him like a father, but fed him, talked with him, told him about Jesus. She would crowd the children into beds to make room for him. Only one of Ruthie's children was particularly friendly with old man Charlie; Paulie was kind to him.

One winter, Paulie and Charlie sat together in front of the fire. "Paulie, if you will call me Grandpa, I'll bring you a little blue dress and yellow radio that runs on batteries so you can listen to the Grand Ol' Opry."

Paulie could just see herself sitting in front of a real radio, listening to music all the way from Nashville, Tennessee. She smiled at her new grandpa and was surprised to see him smile back with a

78

smile so big his handlebar moustache almost touched his ears. The next time Charlie came, he brought the blue dress and yellow radio, just as he had promised.

She jumped up and gave Charlie a big hug around his neck. "Thank you! Thank you!"

Charlie's eyes danced and Paulie felt good because she had made him so happy with something so simple as the word 'grandpa'. She had actually grown fond of Charlie. She had never known her grandfather on her daddy's side of the family since the man died before she was born. She had never spent much time around Lewis, but she had a natural love for him.

Old man Charlie was a sinner, so Ruthie felt a need to see his soul redeemed. She invited him to church. She knew the congregation would be curious, but was not bothered. She learned that Charlie had a great deal of hatred in his heart brought on by the killing of his son. He carried a gun at all times and planned to shoot his son's killer on sight if they ever met. Ruthie and Paulie felt sorry for the man. Although they had never met, Charlie's son was Ruthie's brother.

Eventually, Charlie agreed to go to church. The next Sunday, Charlie sat in the converted schoolhouse with Ruthie and her children. While his attention wandered at times, when the preacher spoke of hellfire, Charlie could almost feel the heat. The preacher told of the beauty of heaven, of the clear rivers and streets of gold. When the altar call was given, Charlie came to his feet. He fell to his knees and tried to pray for forgiveness, but something held him back. He had spent a lot of years nursing his hate for the man who murdered his son. As the congregation prayed, Charlie felt the weight of the pistol in his pocket. Taking it out, he laid it on the altar and felt the burden of his hatred fall away. Not long after, Charlie was baptized in the river near the church.

Charlie continued to visit his daughter and her family. Although he and Ruthie never truly bonded as father and daughter, they came to respect one another and Charlie seemed to be a much happier man than the one who had come to Ruthie's door.

One calm day as Ruthie sat on her front porch, a stranger came walking up the hill. "Are you Ruthie Hensley?"

"Yes, I am."

"I was asked to come tell you that Charlie Spurlock has departed this life."

Ruthie felt sad, but felt that since Charlie had been saved, she would see him again.

Chapter 14

Ruthie cared for her children all her life. After taking on her sister's children following Liddie's death, Ruthie had nine children. Later, she would give birth once more to a little girl named after her nephew Clinton's beautiful German wife, Wilhelmina.

Sometimes Ruthie would talk to Liddie's children about their momma. She wanted them to always remember their mother and know how much she cared for them.

"You see, your momma became a widow at a very early age. She didn't have much of a way to survive so things were hard. Sometimes maybe she made some bad choices, but she loved you. I shore wish I could change all that, but we have to work together to survive and live a life that will please God. We'll work hard raising gardens and putting up food all summer and fall. It will take a lot of food to feed us all through the winter until we can grow a garden again."

Ruthie tried not to worry the children, but she knew things could get very hard for her family.

As Ruthie spoke about their mother, Mary Ruth remembered the cold, blue December day her mother was buried. They had taken Liddie to lie near Josie, another of Emily's daughters who had died as a child. Mary Ruth recalled the chill wind out of Britton Gap blowing through the lonesome pines and how her small body had shivered from both the cold and the grief.

Just two nights before Liddie died, she had told Mary, "Don't live your life like I've lived mine." Mary Ruth was only thirteen but she would always remember those sorrowful words whenever she thought of her mother.

In the corner of her momma's bedroom there had been a curtained off corner hidden by a curtain. Some would have called the personal things hidden there 'junk', but the things were precious to her and her four brothers. The night her momma died, Mary Ruth had gone behind the curtain and fallen asleep among her mother's things. After Liddie passed away, Ruthie had drawn back the curtain and woke Mary gently.

"Mary, your momma is gone. She made her heart right with God, I'm sure. She won't have to suffer anymore."

Mary's tears flowed; she cried for her momma and for the uncertainty that lay ahead.

As Ruthie talked about how their lives would be, Mary felt the echoes of the past pushing to the fore, mingling the present fear and worry with the grief and hurt of the past and the tears flowed again. She was so young, and already she had faced so much.

Did my momma die because of the way she lived her life? she wondered.

Mary remembered a time when her uncle, Samuel Twinam, came to her house from where he lived on Straight Creek near Pineville. Uncle Samuel brought her the prettiest little puppy; Mary had never seen anything so lovable. When he placed the puppy in her arms, her heart had beaten so fast. It was the first thing she had ever had that was all her own.

Her father, Lawrence Twinam, was drunk that day and when he was drunk he got mean. He snatched the wooly brown puppy from Mary's arms. Taking the hawkbill knife from his pocket, he cut the puppy's tail off. The puppy howled so long and loud, the sound echoed up and down the hollow. When her father let the puppy go, it ran off into the mountains.

Mary tried to hold back her cries, but she grieved for that puppy. She had barely been able to hold that precious thing and then it was gone. She could never understand how the liquor could turn people's spirits so cruel.

Liddie and Lawrence were constantly fighting and cursing. Liddie would sometimes become so angry her strength was equal to that of a man. Liddie drank too, but she also had a kind spirit. She had been beautiful in her youth, before time and hardship took their toll. Mary remembered feeling that her momma's soul was dark and troubled most of her life. She had happy memories of good times, but those mingled with other less happy ones.

82

Mary heard many people talk about how her parents had met. Lawrence had come over to Harlan County from Straight Creek. He had been told work was plentiful in Harlan and he came over looking for a job. He got work at a shallow coal mine where he had to crawl in water and mud to scrabble coal with pick and shovel. The 'black gold', as it was called in those days, killed many miners while the company got rich.

One spring morning, Lawrence was heading home after working third shift. He was walking slow, tired and bowed low from crawling in the damp mines all night. He lived in a boarding house up in Liggett Hollow and it was a struggle to walk up the rutted road, dodging potholes left over from the rough winter. The trees were just beginning to bud and it lifted Lawrence's spirit, making him walk a little taller. He realized that working in the deep dark hole of the mine was not a life to look forward to. He felt his will being eroded, knowing that he could die any time from a rock fall or the bad air, and if he survived, then black lung surely awaited him. He lifted his head, taking in more of the beauty around him.

As he rounded a bend in the road, he saw someone coming down a small footpath near the bottom of Black mountain across the swift-flowing stream. He closed his eyes then opened them again, stunned by the beauty of the young woman heading in his direction.

Liddie was walking carefully, crossing the stream over a board laid over the water. Small waves splashed across the board, the water high thanks to spring rains.

Lawrence stood silent as she came closer, taking in the dark, curly hair, the healthy complexion, ruby lips enhanced with lipstick. She was the most beautiful thing Lawrence had ever seen. Liddie came closer then stood still right in the middle of the board. Liddie was wearing her pretty navy dress on her way to the commissary to spend some of the money she made doing laundry for the ladies down at the coal camp. The clothes she wore were her first purchase with the first paycheck she had earned. Liddie was watching the little waves splash on her new shoes, unaware she was being watched. She looked up and saw Lawrence, unable to tell much about him from that distance other than his appealing smile. She remembered where she was and looked down to navigate the board so she would not fall in. As she neared the edge, Lawrence came closer and held out his hand to help her across. Liddie took his work-worn hand and stepped onto the stream bank. Lawrence just stood there, holding her hand, caught up in her beauty.

"You're the prettiest little thing I've ever seen. Where in the world did you come from?"

Liddie blushed, flattered by the attention.

Lawrence seemed at a loss, just staring at her, then he finally got the words out, "How 'bout I come calling on you some time?"

Liddie blushed again. "I live all the way to the top of the mountain and down the other side a little ways."

"It'd be worth the climb."

"I'll see you Saturday, around two o'clock."

They parted then, Lawrence heading for the boarding house, Liddie to the commissary. Each smiling and excited for Saturday to arrive.

Lawrence Twinam

Liddie Smith Twinam

Chapter 15

The week seemed to last forever, but Saturday finally rolled around. Lawrence had bought some nice clothes at the commissary. He scrubbed the coal dust from his body then shaved in front of the small wash basin using the small mirror hanging on the wall to be sure he didn't cut himself. He took his brand new toothpaste out to the spring behind the boarding house and brushed his teeth for a long time. Going back to his room, he combed his hair carefully.

Not bad, he thought.

All week long, all he could think about was seeing the beautiful girl he had met on the road. He had no idea what kind of woman Liddie was, or of the background that had formed her personality. All he knew was that he had fallen for her at first sight. He climbed up the mountain path, stopping along the way to pick a bouquet of redbud twigs and dogwood blooms. The higher he got the more nervous he became. Before he knew it, he was at the top of the mountain looking out over the lush green trees, the fragrance of wild flowers strong in the air. He felt like a prince, strong and free.

He spotted a flat bench of land below him with a cabin in the middle. The cabin was made of split logs, chinked with clay mud to keep out the cold and the wolves. Pulling himself together, Lawrence took a deep breath and approached the cabin. He admired the charm and beauty of the yard with its flower beds and green lawn. But that beauty fell away when he spotted Liddie in the doorway.

Her eyes shone in the shadows of the porch and Lawrence thought again that she was the prettiest woman he had ever seen.

Liddie had never seen Lawrence all spruced up. She thought he was quite good looking now that he was no longer covered by coal dust. His blue eyes stood out, clearer than the brightest summer sky.

Lawrence stepped forward to give her the flowers he had picked along the trail and she smiled. These were the first flowers ever given to her by a man. She had picked blooms just like these many times for herself, but this was different. Lawrence took one of the redbud sprigs and placed it in her hair.

"What would you like to do today?" he asked.

Liddie was a restless spirit, very different from her sisters, Fannie and Ruthie. She had a wild streak she just could not seem to tame.

"Just get me off this mountain."

Emily was out in the woods picking fresh spring greens and Lewis was taking a nap, so Lawrence was unable to meet them, but Liddie did not mind. They walked down the narrow mountain path, surrounded by the budding trees.

After a while, Lawrence asked if they could stop and talk. Sitting on a big rock among the redbuds, Lawrence stroked Liddie's hair and lightly kissed her.

Lawrence asked again what she would like to do. "There's a movie theater not far down the road, I can probably hire someone to drive us there."

After thinking about it, they decided Bardo was too far out of the way and there was no way to know if they could get a ride back when it was over.

They wound up going to a liquor house, the rowdiest one in the hollow. Liddie did not drink as much as Lawrence that night, but any amount was too much. By the time they left the house, in the early morning hours, both were tipsy. They fell into the water when crossing the stream, too unsteady to stop themselves. The cool dip sobered them up a little and they climbed on toward Liddie's house.

About halfway up, Liddie offered to go on alone. "There's no need for you to go all the way to the top. If you leave now, we'll both get home about the same time."

Lawrence staggered home as Liddie climbed upward.

Emily was waiting when Liddie returned home, Lewis was asleep. Emily was clearly upset, but Liddie was old enough to make up her own mind. Nothing she could say would make a difference.

When Sunday came, Liddie was on the mountain. She was carrying her bucket of water down toward the cabin, but took a break to enjoy the colors and scent of the apple blossoms in the groves. She wondered if maybe she should not have gone to church with Ruthie. She looked across the landscape surrounding her home, the apple and cherry blossoms, the slope of the mountain heading down to Martin's Fork. She felt as if a troublesome river was running through her soul. The drinking the night before weighed on her soul. She knew what she had done was wrong. This would not be the last time she felt the battle rage within her.

Liddie bent to fish an apple blossom out of the water in her bucket. When she looked up, Lawrence was there just above her on the hill. Lawrence walked to where she had stood, snagging an apple blossom to place in her hair. He bent to kiss her.

Liddie liked Lawrence and wanted to see him, but at the same time, she was unsure. She felt guilty about what they had done the night before.

"Where do you want to go?" he asked.

"I just want to stay here," she said. "I have the saddest feeling today."

They carried the water bucket to the porch and Liddie introduced Lawrence to her mother. Emily had very little to say and walked back inside.

The two went for a walk in the woods around the home place, strolling hand and hand through the trees. The pure air refreshed them, the spring blooms guiding them along the path. After a while, Lawrence asked Liddie where she wanted to go.

"Anywhere you want to go," she answered.

"Well, let's go get a drink or two."

Uncertain, Liddie called back to the house, "Maw, I'll be back before dark."

"I hope you are, Liddie. I don't like you coming up that mountain after dark. You don't have no idea who might be skulking around in these mountains."

Liddie and Lawrence headed on down the mountain. Liddie cheered up as they walked. As they cleared the mountain and crossed the stream, she left her earlier doubts behind.

It was dusk before they knew it and Liddie knew she had to get home.

"Lawrence, you have to work in the mines tomorrow, I can walk home by myself."

Lawrence resisted, but Liddie talked him into it. She had not drunk much so she was steady as she climbed. The night was growing dark and there was no moon to light her way, so she was relieved to see the lamplight in the windows as she drew closer to home.

Liddie pondered on her relationship with Lawrence during the week that followed. She had not been intimate with him beyond a few kisses, and truly felt she should let him go. But when Saturday came around again, she wavered and dressed up in a red dress she had gotten at the commissary. She sat on the porch, anxious until she saw Lawrence walking toward her, a big grin on his face.

A still voice inside her raised doubts in her once again, but she did not listen.

Lawrence asked her to walk with him down to the rock they had rested on the week before. Once there, he guided her to sit and took his place beside her.

"Liddie, will you marry me? I can't imagine life without you."

Liddie was quiet for so long, Lawrence started to look worried. The still voice was back, urging her to say 'no', but again she ignored it and said "yes".

Lawrence was exuberant, not noticing Liddie was not as excited.

Lawrence rented them a little house at the head of Liggett Hollow and they were married. As time passed, they indulged often in the drinking scene.

Chapter 16

A little girl was born to them before long and Liddie named her Alice. The baby was very beautiful, but they did not change their lifestyle. Lawrence still worked in the mines, and they now owned an old rattle trap of a car and they ran around on the weekends after Lawrence finished his last shift. They were paid weekly which only enabled them to get more whiskey with less trouble.

They would take baby Alice out in all seasons, even in weather too cold . The exposure was not good for the baby, nor were the constant fights they inevitably got into when they were drunk. More than once, Liddie would catch Lawrence asleep and burn his clothes or cut his hair in retaliation for real or imagined mistreatment.

Eventually, baby Alice became so very ill they took her to the company doctor. After seeing the doctor, they lay the baby in the back seat of the car and went on to spend the evening in the usual way - drinking and fighting at one of the local liquor joints. The weather was cold, too cold for a sick child. They went home after a while, opened the car door to get the little girl out and realized her arm had been caught in the door. Lawrence carried her into the house and laid her on the bed.

Alice was not moving and seemed so cold when Liddie touched her. She shook the child but there was still no movement.

"Lawrence! Alice won't move, I think she's dead."

Liddie wept bitterly. Lawrence hurt deep in his soul. They were both completely sober by now. They were silent, but they looked at each other knowing their negligence had killed their little girl. Up and down the hollow, the wailing from the little house could be heard. The sounds seemed to echo from one mountain to the next.

Beautiful little Alice was buried in Liggett cemetery. Liddie tried to think of the good times they had together, but her mind was haunted knowing there were too few. It was now spring and she would walk along the railroad tracks. She remembered the previous October, a warm day when she had stood holding her baby as the breeze moved her little blond curls. Alice tried to capture leaves as they fluttered in the breeze. Alice had laughed out loud in delight.

Liddie could still hear the sound of that sweet little-girl laugh. It was an innocent time, a sweet memory that brought a spark of comfort to her troubled soul.

Chapter 17

The months seemed to pass swiftly. Liddie had another blond haired baby she named Mary Ruth after her sister Ruthie. Liddie and Lawrence, however, had not changed their lifestyle. Two years later, Frank was born and, just a year or so after, Sam came along. As the three children grew, they bonded with each other and loved one another greatly.

One day the children played on the floor with their dog. Frank crawled under the table with the dog when Lawrence came in. He had been drinking and saw only the dog under the table. He swung a chair at the dog, but as the chair descended, Frank moved into range. Frank lay stunned on the floor, bleeding from a deep wound on his head. Liddie picked him up and cleaned it right away, but it left a scar he would bear all his life.

Liddie was angry once she saw Frank was all right. She proceeded to give Lawrence a taste of what he had done to Frank. The fights continued for months, almost daily they would get into it over one thing or another. And yet, afterward, Lawrence would put his arms around Liddie and proclaim, "I love her more than anything in this world."

Lawrence nearly always got the worst end of their fights.

They had one last horrible fight. Their drinking began to slow down and life seemed to be taking a turn for the better.

One spring day, Liddie and Lawrence sat on their steps one Saturday morning while the children played inside. Lawrence had worked hard all week and felt good about having a day off.

"Liddie, let's me and you go walking down where we first met and cross the brook."

Liddie called to Mary to watch after the boys. "Me and daddy will be back after a while."

As they got near the water, Liddie said, "Over there it is, Lawrence. Look at how the water ripples. There's a bluebird singing over on that branch. Maw always said bluebirds bring peace."

Lawrence suggested they take their shoes off and put their feet in the cool water. Lawrence admired Liddie's pretty feet, still well shaped with bright red painted toenails. Lawrence stared out over the meadow and grew serious.

"Liddie, maybe we can pick up and start over. Never go to another liquor house, never fight again. If we don't drink, we won't fight and do foolish stuff."

"Maybe we can be what we're supposed to be; we can take care of Mary and the boys."

Lawrence knew Liddie was thinking about Alice. They both knew their way of life had caused their firstborn's death and the guilt never went away.

"See that meadow over there?" Lawrence pointed at a nice little stretch of land just past the stream. "Maybe I could buy that piece of land from the land company and build us a nice house. If we don't drink or waste our money, we could have enough in a short while."

Slipping their shoes back on, they stood looking at the meadow and the mountain sheltering it above.

Lawrence put his arm around Liddie's waist. "We can make it work, I know we can."

They held hands as they walked back home. Nearing the house, they could see Mary, Frank, and Sam sitting on the front steps. When they were close enough, Liddie took baby Sam from Mary's lap and Lawrence knelt in front of Mary and Frank to hug them. The children seemed to realize something had changed.

Life was so different through the spring and summer. When winter came and the snow started to fall, Lawrence would get up and make his way over to stir the red coals in the heating stove. He laid sticks of wood on the coal to spark up the fresh coal he added so the room would warm quickly. After starting up the bedroom fire, he would go to the kitchen and do the same in the cook stove. The house was small, just two rooms, so it did not take long to get the house warm. Once the fire was going, Liddie got up. After warming herself by the bedroom stove for a few minutes, she made her way to the kitchen.

She and Lawrence had worked very hard to live up to the promise they made themselves by the brook early in the spring. She cooked up a breakfast of fresh ham from the fattening hog they had butchered late in the fall. The winter was so cold; they could leave the meat hanging in the outbuilding with no fear of it spoiling. Liddie made biscuits to go with the ham and fried up some eggs her momma had given to them. She packed Lawrence's lunch into his lunch bucket; ham and biscuits in the bottom, jelly and biscuits on top with a jar of milk. Before daylight, Lawrence hugged his wife and headed down the road to the coal mines.

As he walked, he was deep in thought. 'My money won't be wasted no more. We're changing. Our children will have a better life. We might even be able to build that house by the brook if we can save a little. We can watch our children play in the clear water and run through the meadow chasing butterflies. They can pick wildflowers and bring them to their pretty momma while she's in the kitchen cooking good food for the family. We won't be wasting our money on whiskey ever again.'

Chapter 18

It was a new beginning for the little family. The years of darkness were growing brighter, as if a silver moon were shining on them now. They dedicated themselves to taking care of the three precious lives they had been trusted with. Their children were gifts and Liddie and Lawrence were determined their lives would not end like Alice's.

The winter of 1941 was worse than many for a long time. Temperatures were bitterly cold and snow was abundant. The wind was biting, and the streams were frozen solid. Lawrence never missed work. He was back on the third shift and would make his way through the treacherous weather every night of the week. Sometimes he could see barely a foot in front of his face, but he followed the railroad tracks that ran past his house all the way to the mines. The mines, at least, were warmer than the outside air. Mud and water were still a problem, but they weren't frozen as the terrain outside was.

Lawrence daydreamed as he worked, filling his mind with pleasant thoughts that gave his heart ease. He found it hard to forgive himself for some of the things he had done. He remembered what he had done to little Mary's chocolate brown puppy. He knew he could let his regrets drag him down or lift him up. He chose to be lifted up to become a better man.

Coming out of the mine in the predawn hours, his wet clothes froze within minutes. He was not feeling well when he went to bed, but was not overly worried at the wheezing in his chest; the symptom was common with miners. He slept fitfully until it was nearly dark again, when he woke up feeling a tightness in his chest.

"Liddie, it hurts when I breathe." His words were shortened as his labored breathing cut them off.

Liddie bathed his chest in Vick's salve and warmed a cloth on the stove to place over it. She closed up his long john underwear over the treatment then dissolved some sugar in some coal oil and had him swallow it.

By the time daylight filtered through the windows, Lawrence was gasping for breath. Liddie stood by him, feeling scared and not knowing what else to do. Frightened tears fell down her cheeks as she watched Lawrence take his last breath.

"He's gone," she whispered. "Oh my God, he's gone."

Liddie looked over at her sleeping children, still peaceful and unaware their daddy was dead. Liddie gathered her emotions and walked to the nearest neighbor's house to have them drive to the funeral home in Harlan and ask them to come after Lawrence and they were glad to help. She made her way home, praying the children would not wake until she returned.

Liddie stood by the children's bed and waited. She thought about how they would make it without Lawrence. They had only been saving money for two short seasons, this was the first winter they had stored food properly, but it would not be enough to last long. She knew she should be grieving her husband, but she also had to worry about her children.

When the children woke up, she told them their daddy was gone. Mary and Frank could not comprehend much and Sam was far too young to understand death at all. Liddie just held her children close.

Lawrence was buried in a cemetery at Liggett near little Alice. After the burial, Liddie and her children returned home. Liddie was worried about how they would make it. The hundred dollar social security check she would receive was uncertain and would not be nearly enough to raise three children on. Snow continued to fall as Liddie sat in the room lit only by a kerosene lamp. She knew there was not much coal left and the food was not enough. She felt as cold inside as the night was outside.

She remembered a bottle of whiskey, hidden long ago beneath the floorboard. She thought maybe just one drink would help her get through the night. She looked at her children, asleep in their shared bed. She could not bring herself to cry, could not seek God for help. She had wandered too far to reach out. She took one drink, then another, but her problems remained. Finally, she lay across the foot of the children's bed and slept until after dawn.

The children woke up hungry so Liddie got up to fix breakfast. She knew there was not much left in the house, but determined she would stretch it until the weather broke.

A few days later, the snow let up. Liddie gathered their clothes and tied them in a pillowcase. Bundling the children in their warmest coats, she headed for the mountain path. After climbing for a while, she left Frank and Mary waiting under a cliff, they were too tired to walk further and she could not carry them all. She continued on with baby Sam and the pillowcase of clothes. When she reached the top of the mountain, she could see her mother looking out the window. As she struggled through the snow to make it to the house, Emily swung the door open.

"Liddie? What are you doing here in this kind of weather?"

"Maw... Lawrence died."

"When?"

"About a week ago. Can me and the young'uns stay with you and pap. We can't make it down there. I can't pay rent and buy food."

"Where are the other young'uns?"

Liddie told her.

"Give me that baby and get back down there and fetch them. You know you can stay with us!"

Liddie went back for Frank and Mary, carrying the boy on her hip and leading Mary by the hand. The wind was moving in across the ridge and the walk was even colder. Finally they made it to the cabin.

Emily was already cooking as the family made their way to the big stone fireplace to warm themselves. Emily took Sam upon her hip as she cooked country ham, biscuits, and eggs. When the ham was done, Emily added flour to the pan for gravy.

Once everything was ready, Grandma Emily fed Sam, pre-chewing the tough ham so he could eat it with no teeth. The poor baby was underweight, still not recovered from the malnutrition of his early days of life, and Emily made a vow she would fix that as soon as possible.

After supper, Emily put Liddie and her children into the bedroom with two beds. They all felt safe and loved and warm. Liddie lay awake for a while, watching the snow fall outside the window. Her mind slowly relaxed and she was able to sleep at last.

Emily and the children got on really well. Lewis mostly slept in his chair in front of the fire. He had pretty much overcome his moonshine problem, but he was no longer young and tired easily. Liddie felt misplaced.

Around the bench of the mountain there was another cabin, up the hill a bit. It became empty and Liddie decided to move into it. She felt she and the children needed their own place.

Sam, Frank, and Liddie at cabin on Black Mountain (Mary lying on ground)

Chapter 19

Big John Hensley came calling on Liddie. She had met him when visiting Ruthie down in Martin's Fork. Big John contrived after that to visit Liddie on Black Mountain from time to time.

It was winter again, even rougher weather than the one before. Liddie and the children still lived in the cabin around the mountain from Emily. They were not able to visit Emily often during the snowy months, and the snow was far too deep for Emily to trudge through and she was not as healthy as she once was.

One frigid, blustery morning, after the snow had been piling up for days, Liddie tried to open the door to bring in firewood only to find the door would not budge at all. She tried again and again to push it open, but the snow had piled up against the door and frozen. Liddie tried not to panic. Surely the snow would melt a little later in the day.

Liddie cooked breakfast and saw that the children ate well. She busied herself through the day but began to worry as the firewood stack became smaller and smaller. The temperature failed to rise through the day and the door still would not budge. When she finally put the children to bed, she lay down feeling fearful, staring through the small window into the trees beyond. The snow had stopped and she could see the moonlight reflected on the snow covered branches. With no cloud cover, the temperature would drop even further than it had the night before. She looked at the woodpile near the fireplace, knowing it would not last much past morning. Somewhere near dawn, she fell asleep.

When mid-morning came, Liddie realized she was down to the last few pieces of wood. She placed them on the fire and hoped for a miracle. She sat on the floor with the children and watched the fire burn away at the wood, knowing there was no more to be had once it was gone.

Suddenly, she heard something pounding at the top of the door.

"Liddie! Are you in there? Are you all right?"

Liddie smiled at the children. Big John would save them.

"Yeah. But our fire is getting low."

John found a pick and shovel in the shed and began digging the snow away from the door. After he cleared the way, John pushed on the frozen door with all his strength. After a few hard slams, the door opened.

John worked the rest of the day, cutting wood to supply the house and refill the woodshed. He took the pick to the stream and broke the ice so he could bring plenty of water in for the family. Little Frank watched from a chair pushed up to the window, while Mary played with her rag doll and watched over Sam where he lay on a quilt on the floor.

By the time he was finished, it was dark and walking back off the mountain was not safe so John spent the night. Early the next morning, after breakfast, he was on his way.

Liddie struggled through the rest of the winter. Emily came as often as she could, bringing eggs, milk, butter, and canned food to them.

John had come to care about Liddie and the children. Big John was a carpenter and stayed busy building houses up and down Martin's Fork. People loved to hear him sing as he worked, his voice echoing through the valley. He had been living with Ruthie and Henry, but felt he had imposed long enough and bought a parcel of land adjoining theirs from Roosevelt Daniels. Big John built a two room house across the branch from Henry and Ruthie's house.

John built his house from hemlock, covering the inside with tongue and groove boards. He built a porch across the entire front that overlooked the river and fields beyond.

He continued to look out for Liddie. From time to time he would walk up the north side of Black Mountain. To the old Lewis place and on around to Liddie's. It was close to Thanksgiving that year when he headed up the mountain, the leaves along the path were dry and crunched beneath his feet as he walked. The stream flowed peacefully alongside the path and he felt really happy as he neared the top. When he came to Emily and Lewis' place, he decided to check in on them. When he knocked, no one answered so he opened the door a little to peek inside. Lewis was asleep in his chair by the fire.; Lewis was older than Emily by sixteen years and his age was catching up to him. Realizing Emily was gone, John headed for the path to Liddie's cabin.

Liddie opened the door to fetch wood and saw Big John making tracks toward her home. She hurriedly closed the door.

"Maw! Big John is coming."

It had been a while since John had come by. A lot had happened since his last visit.

Emily went to the bed and picked up baby Willard. He was only a few weeks old, but was a big baby with a full head of black hair, just like John's. Liddie was nervous, unsure how John would take the news. Emily was feeling mischievous, though, and hid behind the door with baby Will.

When big John knocked on the door, Liddie opened it carefully so it would not hit Emily and the baby.

"Come on in, John. It's been a while since I've seen you."

With a huge grin on her face, Emily stepped out from behind the door and stretched out her arms. "John, this is your boy."

Big John froze, his face unreadable. Will was the image of John.

"You shore can't deny this one," Emily laughed.

Big John was a handsome man, and Will would grow up just as good looking.

John visited more often after that day. He loved Will and was always buying things for him. A couple of years passed and along came Esco, another handsome, dark-haired boy. John was proud of his two sons.

When Esco was barely over two years old, John fell sick. He was sitting on Ruthie's porch one day, quiet and seeming like he was in pain. Ruthie noticed and insisted he see a doctor. Henry was away in Leatherwood and none of them owned a car so she hired someone to drive them to the Pineville Community Hospital over in Bell County. The kids were sent to Uncle Steve and Aunt Louannie's house while they were gone.

Come morning, Paulie tiptoed into the kitchen to find aunt Louannie cooking breakfast. She had not slept well, concern for her uncle had left her tossing and turning. She was hungry, but was not sure she could eat.

A sudden, loud knock on the door startled them.

Louannie's husband, Steve was a miner. All miner's wives lived in fear of such a knock so Louannie feared for Steve as she went to the door and opened it. Paulie heard a voice outside the door saying. "Big John Hensley has died."

Paulie fixated on the ham frying in the skillet, unable to take in what the man had said. She loved her uncle. John had lived with them on and off for years until he had built his own house near theirs. Even when he had moved, she could see him on his porch, watching the kids play and the river flow.

Ruthie made the funeral arrangements and Henry took care of the expenses. The service was held at the little Baptist church by the river. Paulie stood by the steps of the little building and watched as the neighbors carried the casket inside. She could hear her momma crying inside as the procession entered.

Big John had made many friends building houses up and down the valley. Aside from his sons, Ruthie and Henry were his only family. Will was only five and Esco three by now.

After John died Liddie and her children moved off the mountain down into Martin's Fork. They took a place over in Britton Hollow at the base of Stone Mountain. East of their new place was the Chimney Rock and a soothing stream. Peppermint plants Emily called 'pennyrile' grew near the house. Emily thought the plant was a cure for just about everything and would brew tea from it when people were sick.

Liddie would set her milk and butter in the water underneath a grove of trees that kept the area shaded most of the day. Once the milk sat in the cold for a day or so, the cream would gather at the top. Liddie would skim it off and place it in a jar where she let it curdle then put it in the churn to make into butter. She or the children, sometimes taking turns, would churn the dasher up and down for an hour or longer to turn the cream into buttermilk with a thick layer of butter on top. The butter was squeezed in cheesecloth to remove excess milk then molded.

Not long after Liddie moved off the mountain, Emily and Lewis moved into the next hollow over. They were getting too old to keep the old place going. Bair and his wife, Mintie Mae, lived on the hillside around from Liddie. Mintie Mae was a wildcat, but Bair was somewhat frail. Mary would sometimes slip under their house when she was bored and listen as Mintie Mae screamed like a wild woman. It was all she could do sometimes to restrain her giggles. Mary saw Mintie Mae beat Bair once with a shoe.

Bair had been ill since before he married with some sort of bone disease. Emily said pieces of bone would work their way out of his skin. The pain Bair went through brought on a nervous breakdown. The law was called one time to transport Bair to jail until he could be taken to a mental health facility. When they passed the church, Bair wanted to go in.

"Lawman, stop! Let me go to church."

The police stopped and let him go inside. Lightning flashed through the window, growing more violent until the little church rattled.

Bair ran screaming down the aisle, "It's the end of time! The end of the world is here!"

The policemen hauled Bair off in handcuffs and he was taken to Virginia. Emily managed to get to Britton Gap and across the mountain on horseback. Bair had been injured during his arrest, as he was mad with the pain. But the police gave Emily a lift back to where she left her horse and she came home.

Thankfully, Bair's mind returned to him after his pain eased. Bair even managed some jobs for a while in the mines and at the sawmill. He put in enough time to receive a little social security disability later when he became totally disabled. In his later years, Bair was a devout Christian unfortunately he was doomed to despair after Mintie Mae became an invalid due to rheumatoid arthritis. Their daughter, Martha, suffered a breakdown but eventually recovered and had two lovely children, Dennis and Clidie Mae. After Martha became ill, her sister Mary Jane took the children to Indiana. She raised them along with her own three with the help of her wonderful husband, Carl who ran their farm while Mary Jane worked in a factory. Mary Jane lived to see all five children grow and achieve a fine education.

Bair later succumbed to his despair and committed suicide. Some time after Bair and Mintie Mae passed on, his step-son, Jess, died in an automobile accident. Mary Jane later died of lung cancer, far too young.

Fannie and boys (left), Bair, Mintie Mae, and child

Mary Jane, Clyde, Martha, Mae Smith (Bair's wife and children)

Bair's Grandson Norman Smith playing at the reunion at Brush Mountain

Chapter 20

When Bair, Mae, Emily, and Lewis lived in Britton Hollow, Liddie decided to take her children and move, leaving her parents and brother behind. She loved her family but did not care to live right near them within shouting distance. The new place was about a mile away as the crow flies. Walking distance, but not too easy a walk. Liddie moved into a one room log house with a rock fireplace. It had no porches but it was a beautiful piece of land. The mountains behind the cabin stood tall behind the lot, several acres of level and semi-level acreage. There was a stream for water and even a small water fall.

Mary and Paulie would play in the water when she would come to visit. They would run all day in the flat areas and pick wild berries in season. The kids gathered walnuts and hickory nuts and stored them under the floor. In the summer, mulberries were abundant, the long purple berries just as enticing to them as they had been to Grandma Emily when she was a child. Beechnut trees were plentiful as well, the small triangular nuts were a lot of work for what little meat they held, but their flavor was irresistible. Persimmons grew on the edge of the garden and they raised potatoes, onions, corn, tomatoes, and beans. When the garden started coming in, they ate very well.

Life was not always easy, but the children never missed what they never had. They even made up their own games, catching June Bugs was a favorite. They would tie a string to the large bugs' legs and control their buzzing flights. The kids would run through the field holding the string as they dodged berry briars and cow piles. This was the most peaceful place they had ever lived.

Liddie still drank and had male friends come by to drink with her. Liddie's cousin, Carl, came by often. Carl was a small man and, one winter day, Frank and Sam lured him into climbing inside an old wash tub. Carl was drunk and sat in the tub, holding to the sides. Frank and Sam carried Carl to the edge of the hill and sent him sailing down, his body bouncing up and down. The boys jumped for joy. No harm was done and Carl walked away, sadder but wiser.

The children knew nothing more; their lives were normal for them. Survival was not easy, but they did all they could because they loved each other and cared about providing for one another's comfort and entertainment.

One day Mary was playing on the floor when she saw something shiny under the bed. She took a peek and found half a hog that had been cleaned, butchered and put into the tub. Liddie had a cousin who was about as bad off as she and the two of them had stolen the hog, killed it, and literally split it down the middle.

As the weather grew colder and colder, Mary stayed inside near the fire more. Her delicate little body did not tolerate the cold well. She sat on the floor staring into the fireplace as the red embers occasionally spit out a little flame that kept her attention. Suddenly, the loud blast of a shotgun startled her and she began to cry,

Liddie yelled, "Look, Mary!"

There was a huge snake on the floor, a copperhead- one of the few poisonous snakes in the mountains. The snake had come in and hidden among a bundle of dried onions hanging on the wall. The boys came running when they heard a gunshot, praising Liddie's aim. Liddie was a good shot and rarely panicked in a crisis. Mary shook for a while, but trusted her momma to take care of her.

The family moved not long after to a clapboard house that would be safer from outside creatures. There was no electricity, but 'juice' was a luxury few could afford even if it was available. The five children were not so worried about the house they lived in, they had the mountains and the meadows, the ridges and the streams. No one would scold them, no matter where they played. They could seek out food and travel where they wished.

One day Liddie was drinking and in no shape to hunt food. It was fall and the mountains glowed with all the colorful leaves. The kids were hungry and Frank was driven into the hills to hunt for things they could eat. There was an old persimmon tree in the woods across the stream. Frank climbed the tree and scooted out on a branch to pick a persimmon that looked nice and juicy. He had no

110

sooner laid a hand on the fruit when the branch gave way, tumbling him to the ground. He was stunned and his head was bleeding where it had hit a rock when he fell. It started bleeding badly and Frank began to cry.

Mary was by the stream, day dreaming as she watched the water cascade over the rocks. When Frank cried out, she ran to find him. Frank's head had a deep gash and blood was flowing freely. Mary managed to pick him up, despite the fact Frank was nearly as big as she was. She got Frank into the house and sat him on the floor.

"Mom. Frank's bleeding; he needs fixed."

Liddie turned over in the bed, not really aware of what was happening around her.

"You fix him." Liddie turned back toward the wall.

Mary put cold water into the wash pan and dipped a rag in. Applying the cold compress, she cleaned the wound as best she could. Surely a guardian angel held protected Frank from worse injury, and guided Mary's hand that day.

Mary Ruth

Mary Ruth and Liddie, shortly after Lawrence died

Big John's little house on the hill

Big John Hensley

Willard Hensley

Esco and Pup

Big John's little house on the hill

Paulie's grandchildren, Corey and Ashley, enjoying the front porch of Big John's little house. After the foundation gave way, the house fell so Ralph and daughters, Edwin, Kimberly, and Jacqueline moved it to their property and restored every piece of wood in 1983

Chapter 21

Time passed and Liddie's family remained in the two-room house. Liddie still had the same mailing since that was where she received her meager social security check. It was not as if she got much else in the way of mail. She would walk up to the George Hollow, across the mountain past her mother's old place, then down to the coal camp post office. Once a month every month, she made the trek over. Frank would always go along and sometimes Sam, while Mary looked after Will and Esco. Sometimes Paulie would come and help Mary with the younger children though they were both still only seven and ten years old themselves. Liddie would always bring back a little something special from the commissary for the children.

Frank was eight years old and had never seen an African American. Several African American families had moved into Liggett to work in the mines. As they walked to the post office, they passed the school house. It was a warm day and the windows were open so Frank looked inside and saw a room full of African American children.

Liddie said nothing until they were on their way back across the mountain. "Your eyes were big as walnuts when you looked in there, Frank!"

Liddie was friends with one of the African American wives and took Frank around to meet her on one trip. Betsy and her husband had three children, two boys and a girl. They also had a fine dog which had given birth to a litter of pups not long before. Frank had dreamed of having a dog for a long time. The kids took Frank to meet them and it was a case of love at first sight. One little pup took to Frank immediately, snuggling against his legs as he sat on the ground admiring them.

"Are you ready to go, Frank?"

As Frank walked away, his heart ached for the little black and white puppy. "Mom, do you think I could have this one?"

"They might not want to let it go, Frank."

"But, Mom, I can tell it wants to be my puppy."

Betsy's husband, Mark, overheard Frank's comment. "A man only needs so many dogs. Little fella, you go ahead and take that pup, I can tell he's already taken to you."

Frank was ecstatic, his eyes huge once again from the excitement of having his dream fulfilled.

Frank carried the puppy all the way across the mountain, down George Hollow, and on to his house. By the time they arrived, the name 'Pup' had been bestowed upon his new pet.

The next morning, Frank sat on a rock in the small field where he played with June bugs and picked berries. He sat with Pup on his lap and thought that as much as he loved his home and his family, there had never been anything as dear to him as Pup.

"Wherever I roam in these mountains, you'll be by my side, Pup. You'll be my best friend all the days of your life."

Frank wished his dad was still around to meet Pup, imagining what it would have been like.. There were times, as much as he loved Pup, Frank would walk far into the mountains and cry as loud as he could. He felt better afterward and was able to carry on. Pup would always come to comfort Frank, laying his head against Frank's legs and whining in tune to his owner's cries. When his inner storm passed, Frank would stroke Pup's fur and smile at his friend.

"I love you, Pup. You're my best friend."

Frank knew there was a God; he knew it in his heart. He knew it when he looked across the mountains or traveled through the meadows and fields. He had heard his mother call out to God in times of desperation.

There were more happy times, than bad, he felt. He had never known any other kind of life so for him this was normal.

A little later, Liddie decided to move again up into School House Hollow. The kids had come to love the place near Ruthie, but they had to go where their mother wished.

Chapter 22

School House Hollow held one old shack originally meant for miners who stayed over during the week because it was too far to go back and forth to their homes except on weekends. No one had lived there since the mine had closed down. It was a little house, built in a standard four-square design. The children adjusted. The mountains were beautiful, certainly, but did not compare to the land they had lived on near Ruthie.

Liddie's health began to decline and more responsibility was heaped upon Mary. The twelve year old worried over Esco and Will; they were so young. She got them ready for school every day, but decent clothes and shoes were always a problem. Once she had to take Esco to school with mismatched shoes and worried all day the other children would tease him.

Frank and Sam got a little free-spirited after Liddie became too ill to keep them in line; nothing mean, but they pulled some dangerous stunts at times.

After a flood forced the river out of its banks one year, the boys found a boat floating in the water. It was a hot, sunny day and the boys surrendered to temptation. They took off their clothes and shoes and left them on a rock well up the bank. They waded out to retrieve the boat, noticing black tar had been applied to seal it from leaking. The two naked little boys tumbled into the boat, rolling over the black-tarred bottom until they could sit. Looking at one another, they realized the hot summer sun had begun to melt the tar. They were covered in the black sticky stuff!

They jumped into the water, trying to scrub the tar off. They scrubbed and scrubbed, but it would not come off. They grabbed their overalls and streaked up School House Hollow. It took a lot of kerosene to get the tar off their bodies. Needless to say, that was their last boat ride for a long time.

As Liddie's sight began to fail, her ability to hunt and bring in wild game became less and less. For years she had gone out after dark to find game that roamed the night. Unfortunately her absences at night affected the children; even into adulthood they would dread nightfall.

A male friend of Liddie's came to help, saying he would see her through her illness. One night he tried to crawl into Mary's little nook where she slept. Mary was very mature looking for her age and the man tried to take advantage. Mary was very high-spirited and put the man straight right away. The man cleared out in a hurry, not making a sound. He had to know Liddie, as sick as she was, would have gotten her gun and made him pay.

Mary said nothing to her mother, but she got revenge in her own way. The man was nearly blind without his glasses so one day she found them on the table while the man was washing up. She took them out near the stream, placed them on a rock, then shattered them to bits with another. The man had disrespected her and she was angry. For days she just sat back and watched the man search and search for his glasses.

Ruthie and Fannie had no idea how ill Liddie was or how badly things were going for the children. With Henry gone through the week, Ruthie could not leave her own work for too long. Fannie lived several miles further up the river, had no husband or children at home, and did not drive.

Chapter 23

Emily and Lewis were now unable to keep their own house. Emily developed rheumatoid arthritis and Lewis was getting too old to care for his own needs. By now, Fannie's boys were grown and out in the world. The boys had joined the military and gone to technical school afterward; Clinton made the military a career. Fannie missed her sons, but was very proud of them.

Eventually, Fannie remarried and moved into a two-story house near a stream with a huge weeping willow that nearly brushed the water as it flowed. Her father, Lewis, died around that time then she and her husband divorced because he was unfaithful. The man was a logger in his younger days then began traveling, drilling oil wells in other states. Fannie loved him and he was very good to her in every way but faithfulness. Fannie was a very conservative lady and never thought twice about putting him out of her life.

The two story house fell into disrepair and her sons tore it down after building her a small but lovely Victorian style home nearer to the stream and the big willow.

Emily had been staying with one child then another, but she felt she was a burden to her kids who had kids of their own to worry over. Emily came to stay with Fannie, who looked after her mother for years.

Ruthie became aware of Liddie's condition. The kids were now in school and Ruthie walked the dirt road up to School House Hollow. Fannie made arrangements for someone to look after Emily so she could help. Liddie was growing more and more ill.

Mary had taken on more and more responsibility, growing into a beautiful young woman. The boys roamed the hills and hollows, escaping the feeling that death was near.

Word soon spread, as it often did in the mountains, and people began to come by to visit Liddie in the evenings. One night, just before dark, a group of visitors was heading up to Liddie's to help sit with her through the night when they heard beautiful singing.

At first they thought the folks from the Baptist church must be there and singing for Liddie. The voices carried down the hollow, echoing through the mountain. The women arrived to find no one there except the children.

The women whispered to each other, sure the angels had let them witness Liddie's destiny once she departed her life on earth. The family was comforted by the story of the angels singing.

Sadness lay over the mountain like a fog. Even the mountains and the stream seemed bewildered by the emotion emanating from the little house. The kids seemed to feel the presence of death in the air. They worried what might happen to them if their mother was gone.

No one ever knew what caused Liddie's illness. There were no advanced medical facilities they could get to, just a kindly doctor who rode over from Catron's Creek on a horse.

When Mary came out from behind the curtain in the junk corner where she had fallen asleep, Ruthie stood there looking sad. Worse still was the expressions on the faces of her four little barefoot brothers as they stared at their mother and filed out of the room. Ruthie asked the kids to go after coal down near the slate dump. Knowing the longer the children had to see their dead mother, the harder it would be for them, Ruthie thought the job would keep them out of the house while necessary tasks were performed.

Their Aunt Louannie and Uncle Steve were there too. Ruthie asked for someone to go to Harlan and have Mount Pleasant Funeral Home come for Liddie's body. The funeral home came and took Liddie away, preparing her body and bringing it back later for the wake. Liddie was laid out in the bedroom, dressed in a navy blue dress with little white flowers. Liddie was only forty-two.

After seeing their mother suffer for months, the children were able to feel somewhat at peace knowing she was no longer in pain. Emily was sad to know another of her children would lie in Britton Cemetery.

The funeral was held in the little white Baptist Church. The little building with its tin roof sat near the river, the soothing sound of the water providing comfort for those in need. After the funeral, the hearse carried Liddie to Britton Cemetery and she was buried near the lonesome pines just as Josie had been.

Ruthie was broken hearted as her sister was lowered into the ground. She wept, trying to console herself with the knowledge that it was only the body being buried. Liddie's soul had gone back to God. Knowing Liddie had given her heart to God before she died brought some measure of peace to Ruthie as they walked away from the grave.

There had already been one discussion about the children while Liddie was at the funeral home so many believed the fate of the kids was already decided. The aunts and uncles sat in the dim kitchen around Liddie's homemade table. The ideas tossed around broke Big Henry's heart.

He and his sister, Ada, had suffered a similar loss and extreme hardship since their mother was stuck in the mountains and unable to work a decent paying job.

One relative spoke up, "Let's send the two little ones to an orphanage." Esco and Will, along with the other three kids, were standing outside in the kitchen window in the cold and could hear every word.

"We'll divide the three older ones among us," said another.

A voice suddenly spoke up, speaking with authority. Henry was not called Big Henry for nothing; he was a tall, muscular man standing six foot three or four. As he stood to his feet, his head almost touched the ceiling. Everyone hushed.

"These children will not be separated. Me and Ruthie will take all five of them."

The children in question were delighted, knowing when Big Henry spoke, no one would argue. They all loved Ruthie and Henry and their kids. They felt like they were, at last, going home. Maybe not the home they had shared with their mother, but a second home with people who wanted them and loved them.

The new family experienced many mixed emotions, rippling like the waters of the stream.

As they each rounded the bend, they could see Ruthie and Henry's house at last. It was a modest dwelling, sitting on a flat area above the road and backed against the mountain. The little white house with its tin roof, full porch, with the stream flowing by spoke of coziness and peace. A refuge for the five little souls who needed it so badly.

An old flatbed truck passed Mary and Paulie as they walked, and they fell in behind it. Frank and Sam rode on the truck bed, clinging to their meager belongings. Ruthie, Esco and Will walked a little further behind, the last to walk out of Schoolhouse Hollow.

Ruthie realized the little boys were nearly barefooted, freezing in the cold winter wind. She had not really comprehended the depths of the family's destitution. Esco had a pack of cigarettes in the pocket of his overalls.

"Esco, get those cigarettes out of your pocket and throw them away. And there'll be no more cussing either."

Esco obeyed, realizing what would be expected of him living with Ruthie and her family. The truck pulled up near the house, Rodney, Harold, and five year old Morine came out onto the porch, waiting to great them. Everything was unloaded in the time it took the walkers to arrive home.

The back bedroom now held wall to wall beds. After supper was cooked and the dishes done, everyone sat around the fireplace feeling tired, but glad to be together.

Eight children were put to bed in the three beds in the back bedroom. The new five felt secure even in their sorrow, and Ruthie's three were glad for the new additions to the family. Mary and Paulie put Esco between them, his curly black hair barely visible above the covers. He was enjoying the idea of having new sisters. Morine was in bed with Ruthie and Henry, while Sam, Harold, and Will shared the next bed down the row; Frank and Rodney were on the end.

Everyone slept warmly that night and woke happy in the morning as they took turns washing their hands in the tin wash pan after visiting the outhouse up the hill. They filed in and took their places around the long wooden table, shining with its green-checked oil cloth. It had not been long since hog killing time, they had pork chops, gravy, biscuits, and eggs gathered earlier that morning not long after they were laid before they had time to freeze. The two families just seemed to click and loved each other so much.

Before he headed back to work in Leatherwood for another week, Henry handed over some cash to Ruthie. "Tomorrow, you hire someone to drive you to Harlan town and get all nine children a pair of artic boots." The boots were rubberized so they would keep the children's feet warm and dry.

The children's Uncle Roosevelt had taken the responsibility of paying Liddie's funeral expenses which allowed Henry more money to see to their needs.

When Ruthie returned from Harlan with a bunch of packages, the kids helped carry them in, excitement overflowing.

"Look, children," said Ruthie. "I had enough left over for long johns, socks, flannel shirts, and overalls. Girls, you have winter underwear too, and you all get boots."

It was not much longer before all of them got new coats as well. They were all set for walking the two miles to school.

The only dark mark on the whole experience was the loss of Frank's dog, Pup. One of the relatives had taken the dog with him clear across the mountains to Catron's Creek.

It was not long after, though, before the boys were awakened one night to the sound of an eerie howl. Heading to the porch, they saw a small shadowy figure down the hill a little way. It came closer and closer slowly then picked up speed and began to run.

"It's Pup!"

Frank nearly jumped off the porch, missing the steps entirely, taking his best friend in his arms once again. Pup could not be still, wiggling and snuggling into Frank's arms.

The other boys danced a celebration for their brother and his dog. Frank was laughing and crying at the same time.

"How in the world did Pup find us," one of the boys exclaimed.

The dog had traveled many miles through the mountains. Pup had never lived at Henry and Ruthie's. Somehow the dog had followed the scent of his beloved best friend from School House Hollow on down.

Ruthie did not allow inside dogs, but she took old clothes to make Pup a warm bed on the porch next to the door. The two friends were together once again.

Ada and Henry Hensley

Mary Ruth Twinam

Willard, Esco, and Wilhelmina

Liddie, Esco, and Ruthie the year before Liddie died

Frank Twinam

Sam Twinam

Roosevelt and Viola Smith

Roosevelt and son, Joe Lewis Smith

Roosevelt's son Estil and family

Chapter 24

The winter of 1949 was cold, as so many winters were in Martin's Fork. Nine children snuggled together around the fireplace, the boys standing in a semicircle behind, the smaller ones and girls in front. The back of their britches legs would get very hot and they would all laugh when one of the smaller children would grab hold of the front of their britches legs pulling the heated cloth against the boys' legs.

The house was not insulated; none of the houses were in those days. In January and February. even the water buckets kept inside would often freeze over in the night so the ice would have to be broken before Ruthie could begin cooking breakfast.

No one complained about the cold; there was no need. They had adapted to such conditions over their short lives. They enjoyed skating on the frozen pond that iced over clear down to the willow grove on Floyd and Jenny Hamlin's land. They would skate in their boots, taking a few hard licks when they would lose balance and hit the ice.

Mary decided to wear high heels out on the ice; the shoes had been given to Ruthie who was not comfortable in the spike heels. Mary was about halfway across the deep pool just above the river ford when her spike heels began to break the ice. Paulie had never seen such hopping in her life. Mary's blond hair bounced as she treaded lightly over the ice, gingerly putting one foot out then the other until she finally touched land at the edge of the river. Paulie rolled in laughter but Mary never cracked a smile. Mary walked up through Henry's Uncle Floyd and Aunt Jenny's apple orchard, out past the skating pool.

The boys saw her limping by rather quickly as they glided between and around the willow trees. Mary did not want to stop; she was still aggravated from her experience trying to skate in the dainty heels. Paulie walked up through the bottom to meet Mary at the swinging bridge. Mary's feet were almost frozen by the time they crossed the bottom and made it home. Mary did not wear heels again for a quite a few years.

The children had only been together a few months when spring finally came. Ruthie had to go off to Harlan to purchase her monthly staples; she would buy 100 pounds each of pinto beans, corn meal, and flour, and 50 pounds of lard at a time as the basis for her meals. While she was gone, the boys had a showdown. Fighting broke out over Frank calling Harold 'Coal Banks'. Harold was pale and generally had dark circles under his eyes, making them look as if they sat deep in his skull much like a coal bank sits into a hill. Some of the boys took Harold's side while others took up for Frank and the battle was on. Harold was getting the bad end of the deal when he spotted the hatchet and grabbed it up. The fight was over. They were sure he never meant to use it, but it doused their anger in a hurry. Ruthie striped a few legs and backsides when she found out. That was the first and last battle between the Hensleys and the Twinams throughout their years of being together.

Ruthie would never yell or scream and very seldom used the switch, but they were well aware her word was law. Ruthie read devotions with her children at night, enforcing the behaviors that were right and good. After Bible reading, they would all recite the Lord's Prayer.

There was no television in those days, but they all gathered around the radio as close as they could get to listen to the Lone Ranger on the radio. The opening lines always made them smile. "Hi-yo, Silver! The Lone Ranger rides again!"

When Grandma Emily would come by and spend a night or two with them, she would often pipe up, "I'd rather hear a dog bark than listen to that Long Ranger."

The children loved their grandmother and were kind to her, but they would never miss an episode.

When the boys were old enough, Henry bought a mule and a couple of plows. One was a turning plow and the other a furrowing plow. Ruthie got onion sets, seed potatoes, cucumber seed, cabbage plants, seed beans and corn, mustard, and lettuce. It was hard work putting the garden together, but loads of fun. They knew their reward would come in late spring or early summer when they could take a salt shaker out into the middle of the tomato patch and sit eating ripened tomatoes until the juice ran down their chins. Summer was surely the time of plenty and the healthiest eating possible.

The children would walk through the woods seeking blackberry patches to fill their pails. They would laugh and joke as they picked, Frank being the chief harasser.

All the children were taught responsibility. They would tend the fields and gather food from the mountains. Frank and Pup climbed the mountain often, hunting and fishing. The boy and his dog had been life long friends; Pup had helped Frank through some of the toughest times of his life.

One day, just short of home, Pup ran in front of a car crossing the county road. Frank grieved hard for Pup, but it was not as sad as the day he had lost his momma and Pup together.

Chapter 25

Ruthie believed God had given her a special assignment. She knew she must teach the children not only practical things, but about the world around them and the presence of God in their lives. She made little moments as they worked in the gardens and fields to fulfill that calling. The children never missed Sunday school. No matter the weather, they would get up Sunday mornings and Ruthie would cook a good breakfast while the children cleaned up and put on their best clothes. Ten children would follow two by two behind the tall dark-haired Ruthie heading for the distant echo of the church bell.

The church had homemade pews that were varnished to a high shine. The boards on the seat and back had spaces between them. As most buildings were in those days, the walls were tongue and groove board. Kerosene lamps with shiny metal reflecting plates hung high on the walls, casting a warm glow over evening services. There were two big windows at the back of the vestibule and on either side of the gallery. The door faced the river and green fields beyond.

Several times a year the church would hold an all day meetin' and dinner on the grounds. Everyone would look forward to those day long gatherings where the best cooks of the valley brought their best dishes and there was red Kool-Aid a-plenty thanks to Harvey Wilson. Harvey would even buy a chunk of ice off the ice truck for the occasion and break it up into two galvanized washtubs. All the children would stand in line waiting for their dipperful of strawberry delight.

Ruthie's chicken and dumplings and banana pudding were always a hit as well. Women like Lottie and Opal Hensley, Florence and Fannie Hamlin, Gracie Wilson and others contributed all their best dishes as well.

Days like these were indelibly imprinted on the children's hearts and souls. Ruthie's guidance kept them on the straight and narrow, and helped them see the blessings all around them. Ruthie may not have attended school past fourth grade, but she was smart in the ways of the mountains and was guided by her faith and her love for her children.

Henry, working as he did over at Leatherwood in Perry County, was wider in the ways of the changing world than those who had never explored beyond the sheltering hills of Martin's Fork, Black Mountain and Stone Mountain. One time a truck from Harlan pulled up and a couple of men began loading furniture into Ruthie's house. It was a nice looking green leather sofa set, end tables, and a coffee table. Something sturdier than what they had been using that would hold up to hard use by ten children.

Ruthie furnished the little house on the hill that Big John had built with two beds and a heating stove. It was an apartment of a kind for them and held special meaning for John's boys, Esco and Will. The kitchen was set up for food preserving in the summer.

They all enjoyed the necessary chore of food preserving. Ruthie would steam seal the jars as the children peeled the fruit or broke the beans, or shredded the cabbage for kraut and chow-chow. They would sing as they worked, their bounty raising their spirits; every jar, every string of shuck beans, every dried apple was a piece of hope to get them through the winter.

A lot of work was involved in the daily struggle for survival, but there were fun times as well. Sometimes they would all gather at the swimming hole and the Hamlin girls: Ethel, Stella, Wanda, Lola, Lois, Angeleen, and Zelma, the Smith girls; Isabella, Phyllis, Oma, and Mary, and Ruthie's friend Opal's boys: Frank, Jack, and Herman Hensley would join them. They would swim in their clothes and bathe with Ivory soap and then swim some more or splash each other with water. In the big water hole, called the Spring Hole, no one cared what they wore as long as they were decent and had a lot of fun.

Bathing this way was easy and economical for all concerned. Ivory soap was biodegradable and would break up before polluting the water. The mothers were saved the chore of hauling and heating enough water for baths. And the kids enjoyed it so stayed longer in the pure water and therefore got even cleaner.

The children would sit on the swinging bridge that spanned the upper end of the Spring Hole, just talking and relaxing as their clothes dried. Then they would cross the grassy bottom land to the dusty roads that would lead them home. After chores were done, Ruthie would allow Paulie to go visit her best friend, Christine Hamlin's house. Christine was an only child and her mother would not allow her to walk alone up the highway to swim with the other children. Christine's mom, Annie, would give them the run of the house and they made more than a few messes learning to cook and bake.

Chapter 26

Much like church, school was quite distant from home. The school lay a few hundred yards beyond the church house around the bend of the river. The school had windows across the entire front facing the river. A big pot-bellied stove sat in the middle of the room to keep the children warm in the winter. The windows were opened in warm weather to let in the cool breeze and fragrant scents from outside. As the population grew, the upper grades expanded out into the church until another room could be built.

Ruthie's children lived the farthest away from the school, they were the first to start the long trek to the schoolhouse near the church. They would trudge up the country dirt road, stirring up dust in dry weather, trying to avoid the mud and ice in the wet and cold. They were joined along the way by children leaving their own homes, their numbers growing as each homestead was passed. Ethel, Stella, Wanda, Irene, Lola, Angeleen, Lois and Zelma joined the procession. Next came Frank, Jack and Herman Hensley; then Isabelle and Oma, then Orville and Dwain. And on it went down the road and up the river.

During recess the children played tag, climbed trees, and played other games together. There were still chores to be done at school though, water had to be carried in for the kids to drink. Cups were brought from home or the kids would make temporary cups from paper. There was a spring across the river and up the ridge a short distance. It was a sulfur spring, but the water was clean even if the rocks beneath were a little yellow.

Angeleen Stella, Geneva, and Paulie were the main water carriers – it was a great way to get out of the classroom. The girls hardly ever headed straight for the spring; when the weather was pleasant, they would wade and splash in the water before finally taking the buckets back. Paulie would fib sometimes and say her momma feared she was getting sick and would get worse if she played in the water; this earned her a piggy-back ride on the shoulders of the other girls. One time Paulie dropped her new shoes into the water and took off flying after them before the current carried them away. The other girls stood in the water laughing hysterically.

When the river was too high, the girls would walk up the country road to Hamp and Cleo Daniels' to draw water from their well. Now, Angeleen's parents owned a general store so she stole some cigarettes and one cigar. They slipped into the outhouse near the Daniels' well one day and lit up. The little outhouse poured smoke from every crack between the boards. The girls poured out of the door and reeked every bit as badly as the smoke. The teacher, of course, realized what they had been up to; Lola let the cat out of the bag. They were all punished, but poor Angeleen was barred from the store for weeks.

The teacher, Mrs. Glenna Dean, was a sweet and beautiful dark-haired lady with olive skin. She knew many of the children had probably never eaten a hot dog. She brought wieners, buns, onions, and mustard to school. The girls helped chop the onions, boil the hot dogs, and put the hot dogs together for a wonderful treat. Sometimes Mrs. Dean would take Paulie, Angeleen, Geneva, and Stella to her home for the night. She had two girls and two boys of her own and would take them all to the movie theater. One time 'The River of No Return' with Marilyn Monroe was playing. The alligators excited the mountain girls more than anything else. Paulie had never seen a movie before; she told her dad all about it more than a few times when he came home for the weekend.

Since the older kids were attending school at the church building while another room was being built for them, they were allowed to perform plays on the stage. Paulie always wanted the lead role so she would memorize the entire play before the first practice.

For Christmas, they put a big hemlock on the stage and decorated it with holly berries, paper chains, and other decorations for the tree. Ruthie, Henry, and the children walked two miles under the cold winter night sky to enjoy the Christmas celebrations. Paulie tried to keep up with her dad, but had to make three or four steps for each of his long ones. Having suffered a lot of ear infections as a boy, Henry was somewhat hard of hearing, but Paulie never minded talking loud, her joy was in getting to spend time with him.

One particular year, some of the students were notoriously mean. Several teachers just gave up and left, unable to control the unruly crowd. Harold was on the frail side and was frightened by the chaos. One particularly bad day, Harold spread his coat over his desk and crawled underneath, singing quietly to himself, "Going to lay my burdens down, down by the river side…"

Suddenly the coat disappeared and he was jerked to his feet. A half-inch thick paddle struck his backside.

Harold would later say, "I knew then that I hadn't laid my burdens down by the riverside!"

Harold was harassed sometimes by his classmates because of the dark circles around his eyes that always made him look like he never slept enough. The kids called him 'coal banks', implying his eyes looked like the coal seams people dug out of the hillsides for house coal. Every day for a while, as he walked home from school, he had to fight Paul who seemed to delight in picking on Harold. After Harold sat on him a few times, Paul would call out to his father, who lived across the river from where they were fighting, for help. His dad would always answer, "What's wrong, honey?" Finally 'Honey' stopped calling little Harold names.

It took a while and four teachers, but finally the wild bunch was tamed.

Morine, Esco and Will seemed to escape the wrath of the paddle. The two brothers kept to themselves, still uncertain and nervous after becoming orphans. Rodney, Frank, Mary, Sam, and Paulie were in the other classroom.

All was not smooth, however; the upper grades had a couple of bullies. The Hensley and Twinam families did not stand their ground very well except, surprisingly, for delicate little Mary who fought many battles for her sister and brothers. Mary would stand up to the biggest boys and came out a winner every time.

One such bully, Clarence, picked on Rodney once. Rodney had an enlarged heart and frequent nosebleeds. He was tall and thin and had no desire to fight. At Christmas, Rodney drew the bully's name and was expected to get him a gift. Ruthie bought chocolate covered cherries for all the children's gifts to their schoolmates.

Clarence was not happy with his gift and decided to take Rodney's on the long walk home.

By the time Mary finished with him, Clarence was convinced otherwise.

Florence, the owner of the country store, took one look at him and said, "I bet I know who got ahold of you!"

One spring day, Paulie was pushing a little black-haired girl on the tree swing. Little Annie was from a family even larger than Ruthie's; she was not dressed as well as many of the other children and some of the other children started to tease the little girl.

Mary and Alberta, Steve's daughter, stood nearby and heard the other children taunting Annie. The teasers were all from more well off families who never had to worry about new clothes or money. Mary had stood in Annie's shoes before with no one to defend her and made up her mind if the taunting continued, she would step in. When the thoughtless children kept on, Mary went for the oldest of the group, Susan. Naturally Lorrie, Susan's sister, jumped in as well. Alberta thought two against one was unfair and waded in to help Mary. Lorrie and Susan had another sister, Betty, and she jumped into the fray also.

Paulie and Annie just watched as hair and blood flew everywhere.

Mrs. Dean had her hands full trying to separate the girls, but she finally managed to break up the fight. Mary and Alberta were sent home; they had started the physical part of the fight. In the end, no grudges were held and the fight ended the teasing. The girls all became good friends in due season.

One day during Christmas break, Ruthie had hired someone to take her to Harlan to shop. Grandpa Lewis was still alive then and was staying with them for a while. While Ruthie was gone, Clarence came by. Clarence was actually a cousin to the family and was familiar with their situation. He knew Henry was gone all week and had seen Ruthie heading out of Martin's Fork. He was friendly at first, but as the day progressed, he picked a fight with the boys. It was hardly a fair fight; Clarence was bigger and older than any of them.

The fight was over as soon as Mary jumped in.

Grandpa Lewis sat in the corner watching the blood fly all over Ruthie's little living room shouting, "Fight, dogs, fight. Fight like you ain't no kin!"

Clarence took his leave and never came back. Mary had left her mark on him once more.

Mary was the children's hero.

Jasper Hamlin, Ethel, Mary Ruth, Paulie, Elmer, Frosty

enjoying music in the mountains on a Sunday afternoon

Jack Hensley, Paulie Hensley, and Frank Hensley in George Hollow after school let out for summer

Angeleen, Geneva, and Paulie - the water girls

Stella, Paulie, Ethel, Mary Ruth, and Frosty

Paulie, Ann, Geneva, Christine
visiting Britton graveyard as most did every June in those days

Chapter 27

Little ears hear everything, the saying goes. Mary had heard people talk over the years and knew her mother had slept with more men than their fathers. She remembered the little log cabin they had lived in once and how Ester's husband had come to visit several times.

One night she sat beside Ester in church and finally worked up the courage to whisper, "Ester, is your husband my daddy?" Mary never feared to speak what was on her mind.

Ester whispered back, "Could be."

Mary took it in stride, learning later Lawrence was truly her father. She knew her mother's lifestyle, but was also sure her mother loved them all more than anything. Liddie would surely have killed for her children if necessary. Although she sometimes neglected them as a result of her lifestyle, Liddie was fiercely protective of her children.

One day Frank was ragging on Will in Big John's presence and John swatted Frank on the backside. Liddie grabbed her shotgun, while she was trying to cock it, John wrestled it away from her and ran. Liddie found it later in the woods off the path down the mountain.

Mary came by her temperament honestly.

Sam was a daring child. He would ride a bull or a horse bareback, barreling through the brush and into the mountains with the other boys laughing and cheering him on. As the horse went under a tree branch, he was knocked off. He was all in one piece and felt good he had given the other boys some fun.

Ruthie never seemed able to tame that wild edge in Sam. She left him to the protection of his guardian angels, she could not keep an eye on him all of the time.

One day the boys were up in George Hollow, working the garden Ruthie and Henry had found to plant. After they finished their work, Sam decided to drive the horse and wagon down the hollow. His friend Ronald went along for the ride. The horse got away from Sam near the mouth of the hollow where the country road separated the hollow and the bottom that edged the Spring Hole. The wagon rolled on, faster and faster, carrying Sam, Ronald, the wagon, and all over the hill and into the field. The other boys ran behind, nearly bent over with laughter.

Those guardian angels had a big job with Sam.

Even Henry enjoyed Sam's adventures when he was home on weekends. Sometimes he would stay in the background without the children knowing and see Sam engaging in some of his more notorious adventures. Will and Esco tended to stick close together, never getting into much mischief. Frank loved his brothers and sisters, but tended to pick at the other children in little ways to get a laugh.

Frank loved his life after coming to Ruthie and Henry's house, but he was sometimes haunted by the past. He found peace as he roamed the mountains hunting or spending time with Pup. He was so proud when he was able to come home with a bunch of squirrels hanging from his pocket. Frank was a true outdoorsman. He loved the cool breezes that sighed over the treetops above the tall trees. He could watch hawks spin and dive for hours, trying to pick off a stray chicken.

Frank and Paulie were about the same age, both of them in their junior year when Big Henry collapsed in the mines at Leatherwood. Henry had left for work Sunday evening, and went into the mine Monday morning as he always did. He shoveled ton after ton of coal on his knees, as he did every day. He tried to keep on with his job, to continue to support his family, but he could go no further and collapsed to the ground, his spirit shattered.

Paulie and Frank went on to finish their senior year. By this time, the dusty roads were paved and school buses came from miles away to carry the children to school. Fannie's son, Elmer, bought their graduation outfits and Fannie made sure they got their class rings; the last two in the box. It mattered not a whit to them, just being able to put those fourteen carat gold rings on their fingers, signifying their achievement, was exciting. It had been a long hard road getting so far, especially after Henry collapsed in the mines and money became so scarce they sometimes had to do without lunch or other necessities. Graduating high school was a huge accomplishment, but they knew their future lay in some city beyond Harlan County. There was no work to be had in 1959.

Paulie Hensley around the time Henry collapsed in the mines

Paulie and Frank, graduation 1959

Chapter 28

Ruthie and Henry's children were leaving the mountains. They were becoming adults with lives and destinies of their own.

A few years before Paulie and Frank graduated, Mary met James Verlin Dilbeck when she was sixteen. She met him one day when walking from school to the store at lunch time. She felt someone watching her and turned to see one of the most handsome fellows she had ever seen. Verlin was doubly good looking in his uniform, his blue eyes shining and blond hair peeking out from under his cap. Verlin's cousin, Luke McArthur, was in Mary's class. She asked Luke about Verlin and Luke promised to introduce them at the store the next day.

Mary walked from school past the huge rock house and church that sat on the hill. There was a train track along the way, carrying the loaded coal cars from Kentucky into Virginia. Although they had heard the rumble and lonesome whistle of the trains all their lives, the kids had never actually seen one before they had begun attending the new school.

Verlin and Luke arrived at the store not long after Mary. Luke introduced them as he had said he would and the two of them hit it off. The pair dated the remainder of Verlin's leave and Ruthie adored him. For two years they corresponded by mail while Verlin traveled in the service. Verlin would come by on his infrequent leaves. Even Grandma Emily took to Verlin very quickly; she loved his quiet, friendly manner.

Verlin was due a thirty day leave around the time Mary turned eighteen. He wrote to Mary and asked her to marry him when he came home on his next leave. He had to wait over a week for an answer; it was a very long week.

Mary was a beautiful girl, many young men paid her attention, but Verlin had captured her heart. Verlin was just what Mary needed. Ruthie approved of Verlin as a match for Mary and helped her plan the wedding. They found an Alden's catalogue and chose Mary's wedding suit. Extravagant weddings and gowns were unheard of in the mountains in those days; no one had money for such things. Mary chose a navy blue suit with a straight skirt that came just below her knees and a white silk blouse. There was a hat to match with tiny pastel flowers and a veil that covered her eyes. Navy heels completed the outfit. Mary was gorgeous. Verlin stood proud beside her in his navy blue suit and smart shirt. Ruthie went with them to Harlan for the blood tests then on to Jonesville, Virginia where they were married. They had only a few days as man and wife before Verlin had to report back to base where he was to transfer to duty in Hawaii. Mary would join him after he was settled.

Paulie would miss Mary's help with the girl chores, but she was happy for her sister. The two had been through so much together and become so close. Paulie would even miss the way Mary liked to torment her weak stomach by taking a piece of fat back pork or something equally disgusting and chasing Paulie all over the mountain threatening to make her eat it when they were younger. Paulie retaliated one day with Ruthie's .45 automatic, not knowing the thing was loaded. The guardian angels were hard at work once again and nothing bad happened. Paulie learned never to touch that gun again.

Paulie had known the day would come that they would be separated and now that day had arrived. Mary had never been more than thirty miles beyond Harlan County, Ruthie had once gotten Fannie's son, Elmer, to drive them to Straight Creek in Bell County to find Lawrence's mother.

When the day finally arrived for Mary to fly to Hawaii, she was nearly lost. She had never even used a telephone before. She was taken to Harlan where she would catch the Greyhound bus to Louisville. From there she would catch a plane.

She got off the bus in the big city and found a public phone to call a taxi to take her to the airport. Mary was an intelligent girl, it was just that she had grown up so secluded from the modern world in the mountains of southeastern Kentucky. Once at the airport, she found her plane and boarded. She had to change planes a couple of times before finally boarding the one that would take her 'across the water'.

Once she got off her plane in Honolulu, she expected to be met by the love of her life, but he was no where in sight. An airport messenger found her and let her know Verlin had been detained.

Mary waited, excited to see her loving husband at long last. The two embraced each other in the terminal.

They found Mary's luggage and were on their way at last to the apartment Verlin had rented for them near the ocean. Every day was a holiday for Mary in that tropical paradise as she kept her house and waited for Verlin to return home each night. She felt more special than ever before in her life. Every evening and on the weekends, they would head for the beach. Mary loved watching the waves come and go off the pristine beach, white capping as they rushed in and out. Mary found herself comparing the vast water to her mountains. It was a big transition for a country girl.

The happiness the two found in Hawaii could not last. Verlin received orders to transfer to Japan. Verlin had not been in the service very long so did not make a great deal of money. There was not enough money to send Mary home nor was it the kind of posting that would make it feasible for them to move there.

Mary had befriended an Oriental girl in Hawaii and they spent a lot of time together after Verlin left. Mary's friend could see Mary's loneliness. She offered Mary enough money for plane and bus fare home, telling Mary she could repay it some day when she could.

Mary was so lonely; she accepted the offer and headed for home. Mary realized around this time that she was pregnant. She was determined her child would be born in the mountains while Verlin was in Japan.

It was raining the night Mary's taxi brought her home. The boys packed Mary's stuff up the hill while an excited Paulie fired up the cook stove and put on a pot of JFG coffee. As Mary made her way up the hill in her heels, the rich scent of coffee was the best welcome she could have imagined.

Mary Ruth and James Verlin Dilbeck, wedding day

Mary Ruth in Hawaii

153

Chapter 29

The months seemed to crawl by and Mary missed her husband terribly as her baby grew inside her. Mary decided to spend the last few weeks of her pregnancy with Verlin's parents, George and Pearl.

The Dilbeck's lived in an old style house a few miles downriver surrounded by apple trees and level, grassy land. Mary felt it would be a peaceful place to bring her baby into the world.

She asked Pearl one day if she had gone to the hospital to have her babies.

"No, Mary, I had my babies in the back bedroom of this house."

Mary decided she would have her child there as well. The culture had changed somewhat, but hospitals were still scarce. The nearest doctor was thirty minutes away at Crummies Creek. When Mary went into labor someone went to fetch the doctor to the house. Luckily everything went well and little red-haired Janet was born healthy and strong.

Not long after, Verlin was transferred to California. He found them an apartment, bought a car, then headed for the mountains to bring his two beautiful girls home.

George Dilbeck was worried his son would have trouble making it in California, but Verlin was confident.

"I believe I can make it, Dad."

Not long after, the little family headed for the coast. Times were good, but sometimes difficult when Verlin had to ship out for extended tours. Mary and the other wives would stand at the docks to watch the men leave, and gather again to welcome them home when their ships returned.

Mary had five children in all: Janet, James Jr., Jody, Jeffrey, and Maria. She and Verlin now have two gorgeous grandchildren: Christopher and Jamie.

Verlin retired from the Navy then worked for the Pentagon for a time. They live in Maryland now, near Washington D.C. He still treats his Mary like a princess. The children live in several different states.

Mary recently survived an aneurism, her loving husband and children stood by her and continue to do so. She is truly blessed.

Mary Ruth and friend in California waiting for their husbands to return after six months of duty

Mary Ruth, James, and Janet in California

Maria Dilbeck   *Jamie Ruth Dilbeck*

Jody Dilbeck   *Jeff Dilbeck*

Sue, Junior, and Christopher   *James Jr. and Janet Dilbeck*
1987

Rodney left Martin's Fork not long after Mary. After high school, he went to North Carolina to work with Fannie's ex-husband, Sid, drilling oil wells.

That winter when the snow was deep, Ruthie received the news that Rodney had fallen from an oil rig. Her heart ached that she could not get to him. Not only were there no family members with cars in those days, there were several hundred miles of snowy, treacherous road between her and her son. A fine young man named Roy Britton answered her call. He had no snow tires, but he did have chains so they set out. Sam went along as well.

Even with the tire chains, the drive was dangerous; they slipped and slid up and down the Smoky Mountains into North Carolina. Ruthie prayed every mile, trying not to look over the edge of the mountains at the ravines they might fall into if they slid too far. It was truly a faith-testing time, and she was relieved beyond measure when they hit level land again.

Eventually they arrived at the hospital. By this time the doctors had stopped Rodney's bleeding,

He returned home to Martin's Fork to recover and met his future wife, Jacqueline. She was a tall, glamorous brunette, very graceful and intelligent. They married some time later and moved to Indiana. They had two boys, Rodney Junior and Russell. Jacqueline was everything Rodney could have hoped for in a wife and mother for his children. She was artistic, intelligent, and beautiful, but also practical, an excellent cook, and a wonderful homemaker.

Once her boys were grown, Jacqueline went to college. She graduated and took a job with Purdue University, but died only a few years later. She was able to hold one of her grandsons, Russell, before she passed on far too young.

It was winter again and treacherous as Paulie, Wilhelmina, and Morine made their way north for the funeral; Paulie and Wilhelmina traveling together from Martin's Fork, Morine from her home about an hour away. The two southern girls were not acclimated to the biting northern winds and were chilled to the bone as they gathered at the cemetery to pay their last respects.

Rodney never remarried; he felt no one could compare to his beautiful Jacqueline. He finally retired from his position as a supervisor for National Seal in Frankfort and took up crafts he had learned as a boy watching the little lady from Brush Mountain who made her meager living caning chairs. America, or Merkie as everyone called her, was much admired for her fine work and Rodney was a very good student. He became a master at making cane-bottomed chairs and even began quilting. He gardened and put up his own food. One year he put up so much jelly and jam, he was questioned by a Wal-Mart employee who felt Rodney was buying a suspicious amount of sugar.

Even after brain surgery, he continued to keep himself busy and now also works for a business just across the street from his home. Aunt Fannie's son, Lewis Hamlin, lives just a short distance away and the two look out for one another. His children and their wives and grandchildren also visit frequently to enjoy Rodney's fine dinners.

While he loved his life and his siblings back in the mountains, Rodney always knew he would never return to his childhood home except for visits. The little school house and Baptist church near the clear river are distant, sweet memories, but his life and his love are elsewhere now.

He misses Jacqueline all the time, regretting she cannot be with him in what would have been their golden years together. He adores his granddaughters, Lydia and Jackie, and grandson, Russell.

Rodney has not returned to the mountains since Ruthie died, one planned trip with Lewis Hamlin, who lives in the same area, necessarily postponed due to unexpected illness. The two men keep in touch which helps both of them feel less separated from their mountain heritage.

Rodney Hensley

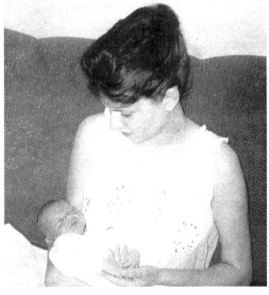

Jacqueline and Russell Hensley

Rodney Junior and Senior

Russell Junior and Senior

161

Rodney and Jackie

Teresa, Rodney, Lydia, and Jackie Hensley

Chapter 31

In 1959, Frank walked off the hill from the house with seven dollars in his pocket that Elmer gave him and a dream to find a better life. As he walked he sang a popular song of the fifties to himself, "I'm gonna be a wheel someday, I'm gonna be somebody." The Fats Domino tune was almost an anthem for the underprivileged young people of the mountains.

Frank was heading up beyond Chicago to Wauconda, Illinois. He had learned a lot about the world from watching the television the family had finally gotten just a couple of years earlier. Frank had no idea what his fate might be, but he was positive he did not want to go into the mines to age prematurely and die before his time choking on coal dust.

Frank was used to living on very little but he feared not being able to make enough to live on. He did not want to return home in defeat. Luckily, he found a job almost immediately in a steel plant and was able to rent a sleeping room for just a few dollars per week.

As he lay in bed the night following his first full day of work, his thoughts covered a million miles. Memories of happier times came to comfort this brave young man so far from home. Frank dreamed of walking with Pup in the hills above Martin's Fork, of snowy days and hard times made less hard by the love of family.

The clock alarm blared, jolting Frank from sleep. He got up and put on one of the only two outfits he owned and got ready for work. Frank had begun work in the middle of the week so his first paycheck only covered two days at $1.50 per hour. Frank took his twenty dollar check to the bank and proclaimed to the teller, "This is one rich hillbilly!"

Frank saved as much of his money as he could and soon rented an apartment. Frank had met a woman and fallen in love a few months before leaving Martin's Fork. Ruby had gone back to her job in Cincinnati, but had grown up just a little further west of the Wild River. Frank had wandered a little further than usual one day looking for a swimming place, finally stopping at the Shanny Hole. As he walked down the hill toward the diving rock, he spotted a tall blond woman. Ruby was as pretty as Jane Mansfield, no doubt about it. Frank felt right away that she would be his wife, but said nothing at the time.

Once Frank felt financially able to take care of a wife and family, he and Ruby met in Martin's Fork and were married. Ruthie went with them into Sneedville, Tennessee where they were married before heading back to Illinois as man and wife.

Eventually, Frank worked his way up to supervisory position, always working six or seven days a week. Ruby stayed home and kept the house, being carefully thrifty with their money so they could save. They had a beautiful little girl they named Donna.

Frank still had some residual fears and insecurities left over from his childhood. He promised himself he would never be a burden on society or anyone else.

Frank and Ruby would spend ever vacation in Martin's Fork visiting Henry and Ruthie, and later Ruthie alone after Henry died. Still later, they would come to Paulie's when Ruthie passed on.

It never failed that in the mornings, no matter where he spent the night, Frank would be gone. His feet unerringly directed him to School House Hollow and memories of the past.

One day not long ago, Wilhelmina was spending a week with Paulie. Around five in the morning, Paulie woke up feeling a powerful need to pray. After daylight, she walked out onto her kitchen porch, leaning on the straight white banisters. She prayed again, calling each of her sister and brothers' names one by one, naming Frank first. When Wilhelmina got up around seven, she and Paulie made coffee and went out to the back porch. Suddenly, above School House Hollow, there was a double rainbow in the sky hanging brilliantly over the mountains where Frank had roamed as a boy.

Later in the morning, Paulie and Wilhelmina went up to Harlan to shop. When they returned to Paulie's house, her husband Ralph gave them a message to call Frank's daughter, Donna.

"Dad's had a heart attack."

Frank had been out mowing an elderly neighbor's yard, had gotten tired, and come back to lay down on the couch.

"I think I've overdone myself," he told Ruby who reached for the blood pressure monitor. When she turned back, Frank was unconscious. Ruby called 911 and started CPR until the paramedics arrived. The doctors feared Frank had gone too long without oxygen which could have affected his brain. Along with the heart attack, Frank had also suffered a stroke.

As the days passed, the doctors gave the family little hope, but they never gave up.

Frank had to undergo speech therapy for a while and, near the end of his sessions, the therapist told him she felt he was still having a few problems related to his stroke.

Frank just smiled. "Ma'am, I started talking like this when I was four years old. I'm just a misplaced hillbilly."

The comment went down in history at the speech clinic.

After a lot of work, Frank has fully recovered. No one was particularly surprised by his determination; Frank had worked hard all his life. Between his hard work and Ruby's money management, he became a millionaire. He was so successful in business, he was asked once to speak to a college economics class, but declined, uncomfortable with the idea of public speaking.

Frank and Ruby have four wonderful grandchildren: Sarah and Aaron are in college; Samantha is in high school, and T.J. is in grade school.

In the summer of 2008, Frank spent almost a week with Paulie and was able to make his usual trek up School House Hollow and a little beyond. He was able to stand right underneath the spot where Paulie and Wilhelmina had seen the beautiful double rainbow they now believed had been a sign of God's goodness and peace. By His grace, Frank had cheated death.

Frank Twinam - just before leaving the mountains in 1959

Ruby and Frank, just before getting married

Shanny Hole

Donna   *Donna and Tim's son, T.J.*

Donna, Tim, Sarah, Samantha, Aaron

Chapter 32

Shortly after visiting her dad in Radford Hospital after too many years in the mines had taken a toll on his nerves, Paulie left the mountains in the summer of 1959 headed for Nashville. Always the dreamer, she thought some day she would head for California to be a model or a movie star. After working as a receptionist for about a year, she finally made it to California. She attended the Patricia Stevens modeling school and worked for a swimming pool company. She even worked as a model for the company for a time. Several months later, Henry became more ill so Paulie headed home.

Paulie had dated Ralph prior to leaving the mountains and they were married. They traveled from state to state for a while following work with their two daughters, Edwina and Kimberly Lynn. Paulie knew there had to be more in life for her and her children. Ralph agreed to finance her education so she and the children moved back to Kentucky. Paulie began classes at Cumberland College, now called the University of the Cumberlands. With help from a wonderful babysitter, Paulie was able to keep her girls with her and finished her bachelor in science degree in just under three years - four months after her third daughter Jacqueline Duvall was born. She earned her Master's in one year and began teaching psychology, sociology, and science that same year at James A. Cawood High School in Harlan. Ralph was finally able to return home and buy a couple of big Mack trucks to haul coal. They built a house in Martin's Fork, nestled in the region where Brush, Black, and Stone Mountains meet.

Not long into her career, Paulie was diagnosed with polycystic kidney disease which would lead to renal failure. For twelve years she battled her disease while trying to continue her job, but was forced to retire and go on dialysis. Three months later, her sister Wilhelmina donated a kidney to her. Unfortunately, she later rejected that kidney and went back on dialysis for eight months until a cadaver kidney became available. She has done wonderfully since and has had that kidney for twenty five years. Paulie made sure her momma Ruthie was taken care of, especially after Ruthie developed Parkinson's disease which finally claimed her life.

Paulie and Ralph have seven grandchildren: Lee, Ashley, Corey, William, Codey, Lindsay Ruth, Hannah Grace, and one great grandson, Malachi. The ultimate pain of her life was the untimely death of her daughter, Kimberly Lynn, who was also a teacher at James A. Cawood High School. Before Kimberly died at thirty-eight, her two older children, Lee and Ashley, had finished school and moved away. Corey was still in high school, but later graduated and moved away to attend college. Her three oldest children were actually her husband's sister's children who had been with her about fourteen years and whom she loved as if they were her own. Her son, William, went to live with his dad in Oklahoma.

Edwina, Jacqueline (who is also a teacher) and their families built their own homes near their parents' home. Edwina suffered a brain bleed much like the one that claimed Kimberly, but recovered. Jacqueline has, unfortunately, inherited kidney disease and has suffered most of her adult life. She is currently part of an experimental study that may mean long term hope for Jacqueline and many others who battle kidney disease. Her greatest hope is that her daughter Lindsay will be helped since she, too, has inherited the disease.

Ralph battled depression for some time. Paulie was left to deal with the loss of her mother, her daughter, and the absence of her children and grandchildren. Aside from spending time with her grandchildren, writing, and helping people in need, her faith is where she finds her greatest peace. Her home is large and open to all her nine sisters and brothers and their families as well as to all the children and grandchildren.

Paulie, just before leaving the mountains in 1959

Ralph and Pauline, before they were married

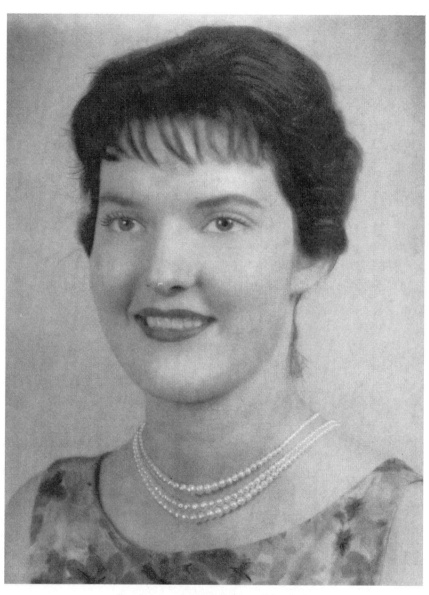

Paulie, just after arriving in Nashville

Edwina

Kimberly

Brian and Jacqueline

Kimberly, William, Corey, Milford Lee, Ashley

Kimberly and Ralph

Kimberly and Will

Hannah Grace and Lindsey Ruth (dressed for old-fashioned day at Martin's Fork)

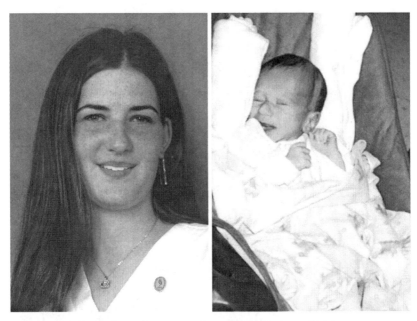

Corey Scoggins and son Malachi, born 2008

Codey

Lindsey Ruth

Will took 11th place in
Oklahoma championship 2008

Codey took 1st place in
Harlan County championship 2008

Lee in his 7th year in the US Air Force

Lee and wife, Suzie

Hannah and Lindsey, camping with Kimberly 2001

Will

Hannah

Grandmother Pauline Harber,
at the foot of Brush Mountain near Wild River

Chapter 33

Sam was something of a late bloomer; he was a couple of years behind Paulie in making his departure from Martin's Fork to the big city. Sam moved to Wauconda and landed a job in the steel industry. Used to hard work, Sam distinguished himself and landed a well-paying job.

Still a little on the wild side, spending his off time in bars, fighting sometimes. He was shot in the leg one night and hospitalized, but slipped out the window to track down the man who shot him. In the end, he could not bring himself to seek vengeance. Eventually, his upbringing exerted a calming influence and he lay his drinking aside.

It was pure providence that he should meet Wilma, a pretty blonde who was also from Harlan County. Wilma had grown up on the opposite end of Harlan, near Jones' Creek. She was exactly what Sam needed, kind, loving, and seeming to know just how to deal with his personality. Sam and Wilma moved to a house not far from Frank on the shores of Island Lake. They had two boys: Darrel and Robin (Bo).

Darrel married a lovely young lady named Jill and they also had two sons, Stephen and Michael. When the boys were still only toddlers, Jill became ill. Jill's mother and Wilma persuaded her to go to the doctor. She was hospitalized and diagnosed with diabetes, but during treatment her potassium dropped to zero and would not come back up. Jill died of a heart attack at the age of twenty-two.

Sam and Wilma took the boys to raise so Darrel could work, but he spent as much time with them as he could. Stephen and Michael are now in college. Recently, Darrel survived an accident that could have been fatal. After undergoing therapy for a year, he is doing well. Robin also has two sons, Tyler and Ryan, who Sam and Wilma cherish.

Like Frank, Sam learned from an early life of doing without and reached the million dollar mark. Wilma retired and they enjoy their lives on the lake shore, but Sam still holds the same trepidation as Frank when it begins to get dark.

In 2008, Sam and Wilma visited Martin's Fork and drove with Paulie to the cemetery where Henry, Ruthie, and Paulie's daughter, Kimberly, are buried beneath the huge oak tree. Following the road beyond the cemetery to the coal mine where Harold works as a guard a few hours a night. Sam had not seen a coal mine for many years and they had a wonderful visit with their little brother outside the guard shack.

Even in July, the cold air flowed from the mouth of the mine to where they stood. The warmer July wind stirred gently through the trees above and around them, but they were still chilled. Sam and Wilma were captivated by the silence; it was so different from where they live.

Sam knew his uncle Henry had died thanks to a mine just like the one before them. Henry had broken his body and mind scrabbling coal by hand to feed not only his own children but five more he and Ruthie had taken on by choice. Their lives could have been so much harder if they had been separated like the some of the family wanted. Sam had sometimes rebelled at all the rules after living fairly wild with his mother, but he knew now the value of what Henry had taught him. He knew how to work hard and support his family; Henry was the only father he had ever known since Lawrence died when he was only a year old.

He wondered what life would have been like if his father had lived; there had been no father figure in his life from the time he was one until he was nine. Maybe he would have been a lot less rebellious, made fewer steps down the wrong path.

Thankfully, he had found his way back from the path of self-destruction. He had his wonderful Wilma, his boys, and his grandchildren. He was, at last, content.

Sam Twinam, shortly after leaving the mountains

Sam, Wilma, Darrell, and Robin (Bo)

Darrell and wife Jill

Darrell and Jill's sons, Steven and Michael

Steven and Michael

Robin (Bo), wife Jeanine, Ricky, Jordan, Tyler, and Ryan

Harold and Sam at the mouth of a coal mine on Brush Mountain, 2008

Willard left the mountains in 1963, following Frank and Sam north to the steel mills. Will was a little different; he tended toward nice suits and upper scale restaurants. He was more socially adept and loved meeting new people.

Will met a northern girl named Jean and married. He fit into her world just as well as she fit into his. They had two lovely daughters, Robin and Karen. Will adores his girls and his three grandchildren: Benjamin, Jenna, and Matthew. Will and Jean visit Martin's Fork annually, and love spending time down in Gatlinburg and the Smoky Mountains.

Ruthie told the story many times of a particular visit Will, Jean, and the children made. One night, after they had all gone to bed, a lightning bug found its way in through an open window. Will called out, 'Ruth! Ruth! Someone's shining a light in here!" A few seconds later, the window slid shut with a loud bang and Will called out again, "Ruth! Ruth! They're coming in!"

Will really misses his second mom. Like all her children, Will misses Ruth's heartwarming welcome, her down home cooking, and her strength when any of her children needed her. Will's daughter Karen loved her grandma so much she picked up many of her mannerisms, such as putting a little salt by her plate to dip her onion in before eating. She wanted to learn so much from Ruthie, like how to make biscuits and gravy. Perhaps this played a part in Karen's choice to become a chef.

They own a camper and take it out to the Wisconsin campgrounds during the spring, summer, and fall. They have many friends who go along, enjoying the campfires, the food, and the companionship of the forest. Will is the number one storyteller, entertaining his audiences with dramatic tales of his life. Jean is famous in her own right for her special cabbage soup.

Will is going to retire soon, undoubtedly enjoying his lifestyle even more. He may not have hit the million mark like his older brothers, but the pleasure he takes in his life is worth more than money to him.

Will prefers not to dwell on the hard times and doesn't talk much about his life in early years. He loves the home he's made with his wife and children in Illinois and does not foresee ever returning to the mountains, no matter how much they might call to him on occasion.

A few years ago, Will's daughter, Karen, and a friend visited Paulie in the mountains. Sitting on the front porch one day, Karen reflected on the fact that she had never seen her father angry. It is a testament to the man that, having lost both his parents at a young age and lived a life of hardship, he came out of it as a strong man who enjoys life to the fullest.

Willard Hensley, shortly after leaving Martin's Fork

Willard, Robin, and Jean

Daughter Karen, age 16

Will's daughter, her husband and children Matthew, Jenna, and Ben

Chapter 35

Esco left the mountains a few years after Will. Esco has a good sense of humor, much like his brother, but found adjusting to city life more difficult. He got a job and an apartment, but missed the mountains and rivers of Martin's Fork.

Eventually, he bought a convertible. It was not a new car, but he loved it just the same. He lost his job some time after and gave up his apartment, deciding to sleep in his car until he got another job.

He told the story later of how he was sleeping soundly in his car one night when a big storm blew through, coming through the cloth top of his car like a shower. Apparently, some vandals had decided to take a nail and punch dozens of little holes in the convertible top.

Esco came back to the mountains, finding a job as a bus driver. He was satisfied with working the land and growing his own food. He was and is a kind soul and found fulfillment in helping the elderly and infirm.

After Aunt Fannie suffered a heart attack and stroke, he was more than happy to help Ruthie by lifting Fannie into and out of bed. Aunt Fannie had been good to him when he returned to the mountains. He even lived with her for a while. Fannie's sons, who lived off in the city, saw to it there was money available for her care, but Esco had the strong arms and kind heart to make practical contributions.

In his early fifties, Esco married a wonderful woman named Bernice. She had been battling breast cancer for some time, but that made no difference to their love. Eventually she won her battle and is now cancer free.

In 2007, Esco had a major heart attack and Bernice stood by him day and night until he recovered. Once he returned home, Esco made his way to Riverside Baptist Church and made his confession, finding a peace he had not known since he was a child. He now lives with the assurance he will see his mother once more and feel the touch of her hand.

Esco is sixty-two now but still remembers School House hollow, the streams, the cry of panthers in the mountains, and playing on the slate dumps with his brothers. He remembers his mother searching the mountains for food to keep her family going before her illness overtook her. The months of sickness that still stand strong in his memory ended in a new door opening even as one closed when Liddie passed away. Esco was far too young to really understand what was happening, mostly he just remembers being afraid because his mother was not doing the things she used to do. He recalls Fannie and Ruthie coming to help, cooking warm meals and looking after him and his siblings. He remembers the wall to wall beds in his new home and his warm spot between Mary and Paulie.

Esco Hensley and Kimberly Harber around the time Esco left home

Mary Ruth, Frank, Willard, Esco, and Sam - 54 years after Liddie's children left School House Hollow

Bernice and Esco

Chapter 36

Morine left the mountains not long after Esco and moved to Dayton, Ohio. Morine has been through a great deal, suffering through much heartache and pain - both physical and mental. Through it all she has kept a strong sense of humor and gained insight into human relationships.

There were only three days between the birth of Morine to Ruthie and the birth of Esco to Liddie. Morine was the youngest in the family until nine years later when Wilhelmina came along. By the time Morine was fourteen, all the older girls had left home. Henry's condition was quite advanced by this time so Morine missed out on her father's attention. Henry was unpredictable, his temper flaring without warning. One day, Morine returned home from church before her mother, having gotten a ride with her friend Phyllis and her boyfriend. Henry reacted in anger, giving Morine a beating with a switch. Ruthie came home to find her daughter on the porch steps, silent and traumatized. Ruthie apologized, but the damage was done, Morine's spirit was broken.

When Morine was fifteen, a good looking older boy came into her life. One day she left for school and did not return. Someone gave consent and Morine was married and living in Ohio before very long. Morine went through some hard times raising her children, she and her husband divorced and remarried but by the time Morine was pregnant with her third child, Lyle, she was diagnosed with cancer. Surgery could not be performed until six weeks after giving birth. Ruthie and Paulie traveled north for the surgery to support her and help with the children. Ruthie stayed for some weeks while Paulie returned home to care for her own children and to see to Henry's needs in the evenings. Ruthie returned home with Morine's children to allow Morine to recover. During this time, Henry passed away from a heart attack.

By this time Morine and her father had rebuilt their relationship somewhat. Being more financially stable, Henry had sent money to help her out. Morine was devastated when Paulie called to give her the dreadful news.

Morine has three children: Cheryl Ann, Lectie Ruth, and Lyle. She has four grandchildren. She adopted little Emily, who was named after her grandmother, as a baby and is now eleven. Her grandson Jerod has lived with her most of his seventeen years. Her grandson Kyle is two now and Collin is six months old.

Morine went to nursing school after her children were born and worked as a nurse for twenty years. Her husband, Bob, worked as an iron worker and is now retired.

When Emily was around four, Morine underwent major surgery. Harold, Paulie, Rodney, Bob, and Bob's sister Gerri were at the hospital to see her off to surgery. Hours passed with no news so finally Paulie called the recovery room and learned that Morine's spleen had been nicked during the surgery and, despite being stitched, had ruptured so she had to be opened again for it to be removed. She had lost a lot of blood as a result. Finally, the O.R. doors opened and the doctor came to explain what had happened. Morine was in I.C.U. in critical condition.

They were allowed to visit Morine one at a time. When Paulie was about to leave when her time was up, the machines monitoring Morine's condition began blaring. Paulie ran for a nurse who appeared unconcerned, but Paulie had a bad feeling. From the waiting room, the family could only stand and wait helplessly as three codes were called over the next four hours.

Paulie prayed and prayed as they waited, then decided to lie down on the floor at the back of the room. She was never sure if what she saw next was a dream or a vision, but she felt she was seeing a circle of stone within which was a bed of red and white gladiolus'. Morine's little Emily was there, walking among the flowers in a pastel print dress picking the vivid blooms. She rejoined the others a short while later, but thought no more about what she had seen.

Still there was no more news.

Paulie called her prayer partner, Elizabeth, and together, one in Martin's Fork and one on her knees in the hospital, they prayed for Morine to be spared.

When Paulie rejoined the family again, she felt strangely hopeful. The doctor was there talking to Lectie and Bob.

"Morine is going to be okay."

Remembering her earlier vision, Paulie was sure that it had been God's way of assuring her Morine would live to raise her granddaughter.

About five years after, a non-cancerous mass was found on Morine's spine and removed. The procedure left Morine unable to walk well without the use of a walker. She was still able to drive, but experienced numbness on occasion.

There was a day when she was driving and her foot went numb, causing it to slip from the brake to the gas pedal. Her car hit the one in front of her. She tried to pull her foot back to the brake, but it slipped again and the poor woman in front of her was rear-ended once more. Once she got her car under control, the driver of the other car came to her window.

The poor woman looked bewildered. "What I don't understand is why you hit me twice."

Morine just sat in silence.

Morine lives in Indiana now. She still uses a walker, but when asked how she is doing always replies, "I'm a strong mountain woman."

She lives in faith and knows one day she will walk straight again and never need her walker again.

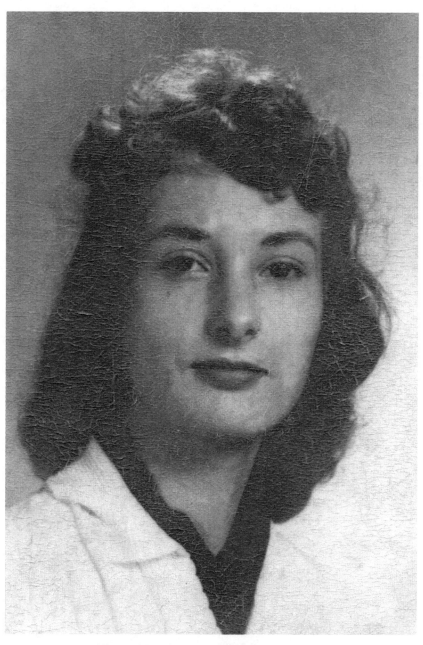

Morine Hensley, around the time she left home

Bob and Morine on a cruise after their children were grown

Lectie

Lectie's daughter, Emily (Grandma Emily's namesake)

Lyle and niece Emily

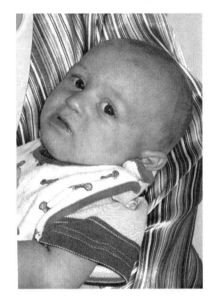

Lyle's son, Colin

Lyle's son, Kyle

Cheryl and husband, Jerry

Cheryl and Jerry's son, Jerod

Chapter 37

Harold attended the local vocational-technical school after high school. The school was twenty miles from home and sometimes he would have to walk if he could not catch a ride. After school, he would come home and walk up on Black Mountain to service the strip mining equipment. Harold was a very self-motivated young man.

After finishing school, Harold moved to Cincinnati where he met his wife Lela, who was from Manchester, Kentucky. Lela attended cosmetology school and Harold found work in a machine shop, but his dream was to become a machinist instructor. They had two children: Harold Junior and Keresa Lynn. When a position opened at the Harlan Vocational-Technical School, Harold moved back home with his family. Ralph and Paulie drove up to help them move. Through hard work and perseverance, Harold was able to realize his dream. Once back in Harlan, Harold and Lela had another son they named Ralph Paul.

They bought a modular home and placed it on a flat piece of land behind Ruthie and Henry's place. Some years later, the home burned to the ground. Paulie was home the day it happened, arriving in time to see Lela safely out of the house with Ralph Paul, the only one of the children not in school at the time. Everything they owned was now gone. Paulie went to the school to break the news, there was no easy way to tell Harold. She first let him know his family was safe then had to tell him his home was gone. Harold looked so sad, but he never said a word. The insurance was insufficient to replace the modular home, but monetary gifts from friends and co-workers, added to a bank loan, were enough to allow him to build a new home overlooking the old home place.

He retired after twenty-five years, but works a few hours in the evenings as a guard at the mines. He likes the peacefulness and the chance to be in the mountains near where he grew up.

Lela still works as a teacher's aide at the new Harlan County High School. They have four grandchildren now: Tristan, Laura Beth, Hunter, and John.

Harold was always a good moral man, but was a little later in committing his life to Jesus. He attended church but would usually leave when the altar call came. One day, he walked out of the church and down the lane a bit when a big Doberman came out of no where and growled at him. He made tracks back into the church. He did not pray that night in the church, but may have when the dog was chasing him. It was later, when Paulie was in the hospital that he finally made a commitment. Harold and Paulie have a special bond and often travel north together to visit their siblings. As much as they enjoy seeing their family, both are always happy to return home to their mountains. Harold's sons live near him and his daughter, Keresa, lives only an hour away in Virginia.

Like Will, Harold is a good storyteller. He sometimes tells the story of a visit he made up George Hollow as a teenager to the home of George and Lottie Hensley.

"I left the Hensleys, didn't come down the road in the holler but walked down the bog field. Just when I got to the wide stream of shallow water, something let out a loud scream. It sounded like a panther. I had a light in my hand but was moving so fast my feet didn't even get wet crossing the stream. I ran all the way home and didn't ever slow down." The next day, he visited Dewey Hoskins, whose house was near the stream. Dewey told Harold he'd seen a car the night before traveling at top speed with one headlight that was bobbing up and down. Harold never let on it was him making the fastest run of his young life.

Harold Hensley around the time he left home

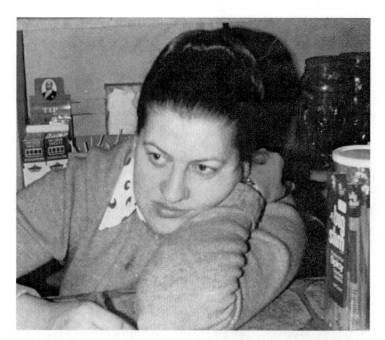

Harold's wife, Lela

Keresa and Harold, Jr.

Keresa's son, John

Harold's son, Ralph Paul   *Harold's grandson, Hunter*

Harold's grandchildren, Tristan and Laura Beth

Chapter 38

Life was different for Wilhelmina. She was the youngest of the nine so spent more time alone once her older siblings struck out on their own. By this time television was available so it was a lot of company for her. She would swim in the spring hole with her friend Judy. She attended the little white Baptist Church up the river and learned values that have stayed with her all her life.

Henry had finally begun receiving the long overdue pensions he had earned over the years as well as black lung and rock dust compensation. Henry and Ruthie were able to buy nice clothes for Wilhelmina for high school and were even able to get her a car when she was ready to attend college. A Mach I Mustang was her dream.

She headed to Dayton, Ohio where Morine and Bob lived. Bob was happy to help Wilhelmina find her dream car. Unfortunately, her only experience driving a car had been driver's ed in high school since her parents did not own a car for her to practice in. After purchasing the Mustang, Wilhelmina practiced driving it in a huge parking lot. She had never experienced a stick shift. Feeling confident, she headed back home driving the Mustang. Not only making her first long trip driving, it was also her first time driving a manual. She would forget to take her foot off the clutch and left many black streaks down I-75 on her way home. She noticed the car was jerking a great deal. The police must have been very busy elsewhere that day because she drove the entire way without being stopped once. Of course, by the time she reached home, Wilhelmina had mastered the art of clutch and shift.

Mary's daughter, Janet, was visiting at the time so Wilhelmina convinced her to go out for a drive.

"Let's head over to the park at Crank's Creek and see if my friend Josh is there." He was, but with another girl.

Showing off, Wilhelmina gunned the Mustang a little too much in the gravel by the roadside. The gravel scattered, the car fish-tailed, then went airborne. They landed in a grassy field, still on all four tires, but they heard glass breaking and bumped their heads on the car roof. Wilhelmina drove out of there smiling as if she had meant to do all that. When they reached home, Henry was lying under the huge silver maple near the drive. She was feeling guilty by now and was afraid her dad might see damage under the car from his vantage point. She had not stopped to check on the way home. She later told Paulie, "I was so relieved when Dad never uttered a word. If anything had been wrong under there, he would have seen it from where he was. I still don't know where the glass came from!"

Wilhelmina left home a few weeks later, but only as far as Morehead State University just east of Lexington. Although she attended college, she never pursued a career. Wilhelmina became a homemaker and full-time mother. Her husband, Freddy, works with his brothers across many states turfing sports facilities. She had one son, J.R., who is now thirty-two and the spitting image of his grandfather, Big Henry. J.R. worked a few years with his father and uncles, before settling in Morehead and becoming a welder.

Wilhelmina and her husband live in a beautiful farmhouse they refurbished about four hours away from Martin's Fork. Sitting on a mostly cleared ninety acres near the ridge, they have a world of their own there. They hope, someday, J.R. will meet someone, marry, and give them grandchildren.

When she comes to Martin's Fork to visit, she and Paulie spend time together, walking by the river where Wilhelmina captures the abundant natural beauty with her camera.

As the next youngest girl, Paulie was thirteen when Wilhelmina was born. Paulie helped her mother out by taking care of her baby sister. Wilhelmina looked at Paulie as her 'little momma' and Ruthie as her 'big momma'. The two still laugh over the time when Wilhelmina was toddling around the house while Paulie was shoveling the ashes from the grate. Out of no where came a sharp whack to the side of her head. Her angelic baby sister had taken up the fireplace poker and was staring at it as if not entirely certain what she had just done. Paulie kept a closer eye on her little sister from then on, and the poker. Neither of them could have imagined in that moment that some day Wilhelmina would risk her life to save her sister. Never could a bond be greater.

216

At the holidays, Wilhelmina, Freddy, and J.R. enjoy coming to Paulie's house. The big family atmosphere takes them all back to their younger days. Paulie and her husband always have a big tree in the great room. Many families gather in and Wilhelmina enjoys those times she did not always have as a child because the others were so much older than she.

Wilhelmina and Paulie drive by the old home place sometimes and on up to the cemetery where Ruthie, Henry, Kimberly, and little Ruby Mae lie at rest. They sit on the bench there and absorb the peace as the sun shimmers across the mountains, lighting the rippling water into sparks of dancing light. They talk of the good times and the laughter of those who have gone before. They share the hope they one day will be reunited in a land of beauty that will even surpass that which they know on Earth.

Wilhelmina Hensley just before leaving for college

Wilhelmina, husband Freddy, son J.R.

Wilhelmina, Freddie, and J.R. enjoy Christmas down home at Martin's Fork every year with the Harber family and more

Behind the house

Codey and William

Freddie, J.R., Wilhelmina

Brian, Hannah, Lindsay

Edwina and Paulie

William, Lee, Corey, and Ashley

Wilhelmina

Paulie, shortly before receiving Wilhelmina's kidney

Wilhelmina and Pauline after the transplant

Chapter 39

All ten children are blessed; all are still living and able to enjoy their lives.

Come October when the air is just cool enough to enjoy and the mountains filled with every color imaginable, they plan a reunion at Paulie's home, snuggled beneath Stone Mountain. Tables with autumn colored cloths will be placed on the porches and decks and the back yard and overloaded with food.

They will talk of the present and the past, and enjoy being surrounded by their beautiful mountains with the rock formations they have known all their lives still standing sentinels over the valley, weathering every storm just as the Hensley's and Twinam's have done over the years.

There will be over sixty in attendance if everyone is able to attend. Those who have gone before will be missed and remembered.

No doubt the family will wonder what Grandma Emily would think if she was still here, riding through Britton gap around the mountain to look down on Ruthie's clan. Would she think to herself, none of that awesome bunch would even be down there having a big time if not for me." Would she be stunned to see how time has made a change to the pristine land she knew?

Emily was one of a kind. Life was hard for her, but the mountains brought peace to her soul just as they bring peace to us, her people, generation after generation.

Table Rock

Chimney rock in Stone Mountain

Black Mountain across Martin's Fork River

Paulie and Ralph's house

Sam, Frank, Wilhelmina, Morine, Harold, Paulie (seated)

Reunion preceding Ruthie's death
Front: Morine, Wilhelmina, Mary Ruth, Paulie
Back: Willard, Frank, Esco, Ruthie, Harold, Sam, Rodney

Sam, Ralph, Kimberly, Rodney

Rodney

Harold and Frank

Brian, Jackie, Steven, and Jeanine

Part of Family at Reunion 2008

Wilhelmina, Reunion 2008

Harold and grandson Hunter

Part of Ruthie's grandchildren

CPSIA information can be obtained at www.ICGtesting.com
Printed in the USA
LVOW111313090911

245479LV00005BA/45/P

9 780982 396902